Coming Home: A Pilgrim's Guide to Living the Medjugorje Messages

J.M.J.

Cover Design and Formatting: Darcie Nielsen

Dedication

To the Infant Jesus of Prague & the Blessed Virgin Mary
and
To Christian

Contents

Introduction   7

1. Dear Friend   11

    Photos   27

2. Let's not forget   31

3. Start here   33

4. Just because you've changed...   43

5. Stuff, stuff and more stuff   49

6. Heaven on earth   65

7. Speaking with God   73

8. Where's home?   85

9. Another Nazareth   95

10. Your best friends   103

11. I'm sorry   111

12. How much is too much?   119

13. Mama!   125

14. For fun   133

Conclusion   147

Epilogue   151

Acknowledgments   153

Introduction

Coming home from Medjugorje is difficult. You have just experienced heaven on earth and you're still processing it. You feel so different, yet everything around you has stayed the same. Your commitments and schedule pull for your attention and you feel like you're losing your sense of peace. People ask you what it was like. You just don't have the words. How do you describe feeling so profoundly loved by Jesus and Mary? The sun spinning? The overwhelming peace? The most beautiful Mass? The most honest confession? Kneeling in Adoration? The secrets being secrets? The treacherous climb up Cross Mountain? The people whom you met and what you learned? The coincidences that were, in fact, Divine Providence? You can only seem to say, "You have to go for yourself," which leaves them irritated and annoyed.

The Roman Catholic Church approaches private revelations with great care and caution. It must be first understood what the Church teaches about Revelation: Christ is the fullness of the Revelation. Private revelations are not to add or compete with Christ's revelation, which is why belief in private revelations is not required to have the fullness of the faith. That is not to say that approved private revelations don't have their own place in the Church. Approved private revelations are received as help for the faithful to live out Christ's revelation in that specific time in history. Throughout history, the Church has been guided by the magisterium in discernment, and with her authority has approved a number of private revelations to be worthy of belief. (CCC #67).

Medjugorje is a small town in Bosnia-Herzegovina in which six children claimed to have apparitions of Our Lady, starting in 1981 up until the present day. The visionaries, who are now adults, have shared messages from Our Lady (private and public) for the past 37 years. Our Lady has entrusted ten secrets to three of the visionaries, who now only see her once a year or once a month. The other three visionaries have nine of the ten secrets and still claim to have apparitions with her daily. A book recommendation for more information on the apparitions of Our Lady of Medjugorje are "*The Visions of the Children*" by Janice T. Connell and "*My Heart Will Triumph*" – an autobiography by visionary Mirjana Soldo.

On May 17, 2017 the Ruini Commission, which was established by Pope Benedict XVI in 2010 to investigate Medjugorje, released the result of a vote that approved the first seven days of the apparitions in 1981. The result of the remaining days has yet to be released. Pope Francis commented that, in his personal opinion, he didn't think the Madonna was like the post-master giving messages at a specific time each day. Although, Pope Francis did acknowledge changes in the lives of people who go to Medjugorje, and he commissioned Archbishop Henryk Hoser of the Diocese of Warszawa-Praga, Poland to evaluate the pastoral needs of Medjugorje.

I am encouraged by the teachings of Mother Church. In my opinion, the times we are living in are pivotal and the private revelations of Our Lady of Medjugorje are helping the faithful live out Christ's revelation. I trust that the Holy Spirit is guiding the investigation process; and the Church will make a further decision at the appropriate time. I do not worry either way because I know what Our Lady of Medjugorje has done and continues to do for me. I can only repeat Jesus' words, "So by their fruits you will know them" (Matthew 7:20).

You know you were meant to go to Medjugorje, but were you meant to come home? That's what it feels like, and it's difficult.

This book is necessary because when we come back from Medjugorje and try to live the messages, we struggle. We are processing it and living it at the same time. We find ourselves saying too much, and then too little. We have questions about how to fast. We want to pray with the heart, but we pray the rosary with our lips while our minds wander. We wonder why more people aren't talking about Medjugorje. We sometimes get a little scrupulous and feel more like a hypocrite in trying to fulfill Our Lady's messages. This book is about returning from our pilgrimage — a practical guide to living the five stones with anecdotes to reassure you that you're not alone in answering Our Lady's call. The five stones were given by Our Lady to help us defeat sin and darkness, just as David gathered five small stones to kill Goliath. The five stones are prayer, specifically the rosary, fasting on bread and water Wednesdays and Fridays, monthly Confession, Holy Mass, and reading Scripture daily.

For those who haven't been to Medjugorje or cannot go to Medjugorje, this book is still for you. You've experienced your own "Medjugorje" — an encounter with the Divine and a desire to change your life. You've experienced God's love and want to love Him in return. Maybe it happened on another pilgrimage or in a life event or maybe just Sunday Mass at your home parish. All that matters is that you are here, right now, at this point. The source is the same: Almighty God. The call is the same: to be holy. The foundation to answer the call is the same: prayer, fasting, Confession, Holy Mass and Scripture. By going deeper in living the five stones, we will be inspired to follow God's plan for us. Our hearts will be ready to say "yes" to whatever He calls us to do.

"When you look for me, you will find me. Yes, when you seek me with all your heart, I will let you find me—oracle of the LORD—and I will change your lot..." (Jeremiah 29: 13-14).

Dear Friend

Chapter 1

I've been trying to live the Medjugorje messages since my first pilgrimage in June 2010. I've been trying to pray, to fast on bread and water on Wednesdays and Fridays, to read Scripture daily, to participate in daily Mass, and to go to Confession monthly. I say "try" because I'm still a student in Our Lady's school of love. I must tell you up front that on my first pilgrimage to Medjugorje, I told Our Lady, *I just want to work for you. I'll do anything for you!* She took me at my word and this book is one of her projects for me. She placed the desire to write a book in my heart after my first pilgrimage, and now eight years later, Our Lady has given me the confirmation and grace to write it.

I don't like this part, but I know you will. I'm going to share with you my "before" and "after" stories of going to Medjugorje. Medjugorje has a way of doing that. I hope it reminds you of what God's grace and the powerful intercession of Our Lady can do.

It started with my baptism into the Catholic Church. On that day, I was claimed for Jesus Christ and anointed with the Holy Spirit, making me an adopted daughter of God. I thank my parents for handing this great gift of faith on to me at such a young age. It is because of my baptism that, no matter how far I wandered from God in my later life, He would always chase after me and bring me back.

My upbringing was pretty typical of an American girl in a small town outside of Boston (minus the couple years spent overseas for my dad's work). I lived in a safe neighborhood full of kids, played soccer, and visited my grandparents and extended family members often. I loved school, my teachers, and my friends. My parents loved one another and laughed together. The one time I remember them raising their voices, I ran upstairs and called my neighbor for fear that they were getting a divorce. But, of course, that wasn't happening. Even my brother and I were best friends. We had our moments, as siblings do, but we were a team and always had each other's back. In our home, peace and love abounded. Life was beautiful and God's blessings surrounded me.

Looking back, I recognize that I had quite a wonderful prayer life growing up. I was blessed to have religious education teachers (including my mom) who awakened my faith at a young age, and who made Catholicism come alive for me when they talked about the angels as our guardians and the saints as our friends. There's a picture of me as a four-year-old drinking the water at Lourdes. It's like my whole being had a thirst for Jesus. I remember preparing for my First Holy Communion and even my first confession. One Lent, our church handed out small crowns of thorns. I slid one onto my index finger, and it fit perfectly. I remember thinking to myself, *I never want to take this off. I always want to be reminded of what Jesus went through.* I have memories of praying at night in my room and thanking Jesus for dying on the cross for me; in fact, telling him how much I loved him often brought me to tears.

One afternoon, while I was praying alone in my room, I experienced a particularly powerful and moving encounter with Our Lord. I was about eight years old at the time and I remember thinking, *He's so close to me. I really can ask Him anything.* Summoning my courage, I asked, "God, will I go to heaven?" I waited, but there was only silence. I continued asking him, over and over. Again in tears, I cried out, "God, I need to know! Please tell me! Will I go to heaven?" His voice filled my room and resonated through my body. Loud and clear I heard, "Yes, you will come to heaven to me." I wept in gratitude.

The time we spent overseas in Geneva, Switzerland made a lasting impression on me. To this day, I still find myself talking about the experience even though it lasted just two years, between the ages of 8 and10. Attending an international school, I learned about other countries, cultures, and languages. I was the only American in my class. During this period, witnessing the diversity of backgrounds and experiences, I gained a greater respect for others. My peers were all so interesting. No one resembled anyone I knew in the U.S. Weekends were spent skiing or hiking, depending on the season. My love for nature grew during these months, and I experienced God through the beauty of mountainous landscapes, glaciers, lakes, and rivers.

Back home in Massachusetts, I settled in just fine and life continued as before, full of joy and blessings. In 2002, the news of the clergy abuse crisis broke here in Boston. It shook my family's faith, as it did many families in the Church. As I was only 12 years old at the time, I didn't fully understand what had happened, and yet I saw how upset my parents were. Perhaps what hurt them the most is that the cardinal, a very charismatic and joyful man, had come to visit our parish just a few weeks before. When the crisis broke, they felt utterly betrayed. We didn't go to Mass for a period of time. Our family tried to fill the void by attending a Methodist church one Sunday, but we never returned; there was something missing. Eventually, we began to attend Sunday Mass at our Catholic parish once again. But it was clear that my family had changed. My parents were, shaken by the crisis, but knew faith was important and were committed to raising us in it. As a parent myself now, I can understand their pain.

Before long I was in high school, and at this time something in me changed drastically. Was it my friends? The culture? The breakdown of my faith? My own weakness? A combination of all these things? All I know is that I wanted to fit in. I wanted to be liked and I was willing to sacrifice for this end. People already liked me as I was, but for some strange reason, I felt I should be different. I wanted to prove myself. In my teenage head, I concluded that if I excelled in school and sports, then I could pull off what I wanted on the side. My parents had taught me the value of self-discipline and a strong work ethic. It was in my nature to give 110% in everything I undertook. Somehow, loyalty and my love of God and his commandments slipped out of my mind and sank to the bottom of my heart.

At 14, I was introduced to alcohol by some older kids. Not only did I love the freedom alcohol gave me, but also the sneaking, stealing and finding ways to get it was just as "fun." My parents noticed a change and even caught me a couple times. There were punishments and consequences, but I somehow now enjoyed "being bad." I was reckless and didn't care if I hurt them with my actions or words. Nevertheless, during these years I continued going to Sunday Mass. I had stopped going to confession and our culture didn't promote it — especially after the crisis. But by God's grace, through Holy Mass there was still goodness growing in me, with a desire for more, even though I had found comfort in the darkness.

I was under the assumption that everyone went through wild years at some point. I chose mine to be high school. Junior year was particularly difficult because my relationship with my mom was strained. I really challenged my relationship with my mother. Perhaps all girls do this at some point, but I think I really sank a dagger into my mom's heart because she and my dad worked really hard to be, and were, great parents. My confirmation was approaching and at that time, I didn't see the point of it. I almost backed out, but knowing extended family would be there I didn't want to disappoint them.

My parents tried to get me out of public school by having me apply to one of the private Catholic all-girls' schools. In my rebellion and not wanting to leave, I purposely failed the entrance exam. My mom had a feeling I did that because I was an honor-roll student. It wasn't until years later that I confirmed it.

I became depressed, naturally, because I was doing everything that deep down I didn't want to do. I was becoming the very person that in my heart I didn't want to become. I drank more because alcohol was my way to numb the pain and restlessness. I wanted to escape. My mom saw the pain in me and wanted to help.

It is only in looking back that we realize that "healing" can be a wolf in sheep's clothing. Thinking that I needed some sort of spiritual breakthrough, I naively became involved with the occult — Reiki, palm reading, fortune telling — you name it. I got involved and I wasn't healed. No, I got worse. I had lost the fear of death in a bad way. I applied my 110% mentality to drinking: I'd only do it if I could get drunk. I must also add that hatred took deep root in my heart — hatred especially towards my parents. In my head, and only there, they were limiting my freedom, and it was their fault I was doing what I was doing.

Just how far I had fallen was revealed during my junior year, when the police broke up a party I attended. After my parents picked me up and brought me home, I was furious. I was mad at myself, but I took it out on them. I said I didn't have to stay and that I was leaving. As I walked across the lawn, my dad yelled from the front door that if I stepped off the property he would call the cops. Yeah, right, I thought. I went to a neighbor's and he said my dad called and asked him to send me home. Realizing I really had no where to go and that it was a cold night, I went home. Without saying anything to my parents I went up to my room and slammed the door.

A few minutes later, there was a knock. My mom said, "Darcie, there's someone here to see you." I went downstairs, turned the corner, and there in our home were two police officers. My heart was in my throat. My own father actually called the cops on me. I'm not proud of what I did that night, and I respect my dad for following through on his word. The officers had me sit down and explained that because I was under 18, I was still a minor and had to obey what my parents said. My brother, who was only 13 at the time, reflected years later that he felt like he was on the Cops show because he had just gotten out of the shower when they arrived and didn't know what was going on. Like the younger siblings on the show, he "stayed in his room." Needless to say, this incident resulted in community service (as required by the judge) and a short-term suspension from my tennis team in the spring. The secret was out: Darcie wasn't as innocent as she seemed.

During the fall of my senior year, it was God's intervention that brought a wonderful young man into my life. We started dating and I was immediately blessed to see how his family lived the Catholic faith. I had wonderful examples in my own family, from my parents to grandparents, aunts and uncles, and yet it often takes an outside witness for us to take notice. God gave me this through this relationship. I admired my boyfriend's older sister who was in college studying ministry. She had a long-term boyfriend and they planned to get married. Through them, I was being drawn back into the faith. I had started journaling and was rediscovering my relationship with God. Being told I was "very special" and that there was something "beautiful about my soul" were the words of truth that I so desperately longed for and needed to hear. Again, this message was given to me by my family's love, but I was deaf to it. I was beginning to live differently and had even given up drinking. Peace was being restored to my life. God was at work.

The relationship with the young man continued into college, but the school introduced a new setting, especially being located in Boston. The city was our campus. I made friends easily in the dorms, including becoming close friends with a Muslim girl who also didn't drink, which we bonded over. In a short time, our group of friends grew beyond our dorm and included friends from other colleges and universities. Drinking was eventually re-introduced. I remember thinking, *I'm in control* and, for the most part, I didn't abuse alcohol like I had in high school.

During Lent of sophomore year of college, I made the resolution to attend Mass more than just on Sunday. There was a chapel within walking distance with an 8 a.m. Mass Tuesday through Thursday. It seemed early at the time, but I did it anyway. It started with one day a week, and I gradually added as many days as my class schedule would allow. Again, this was God's grace nourishing me in the Eucharist and sustaining me.

One day during November of my junior year in college, I received terrible news. My 30-year-old cousin, Renee, and her two-year-old daughter, Emily, died in a car accident. They were on their way to see the husband's mother, who had just died. It was a shock to our family and brought us into deep mourning. We cried, and we cried hard. Words were inadequate. Consoling came through hugs, tears and prayers. I remember my aunt, who was the mother and grandmother, saying that when she walked into church she told God, "Even though this happened, I am not giving up my faith." This has always stuck with me. Even in the face of the most horrible tragedy, she had the grace to still believe and trust in God.

At the luncheon gathering after the Funeral Mass, we saw extended family members that we normally wouldn't see. I was talking with my great aunt and uncle, and they started to tell me about a place called Medjugorje. It came up naturally in conversation, and they shared it with such confidence and normality that I was perplexed. Why wasn't this bigger news? I was so intrigued, perhaps looking still for the spiritual breakthrough I sought years before. The Virgin Mary appearing on earth? This was miraculous to me. A seed of hope was planted deep in my heart, and I knew I had to go. It was like I had been waiting my whole life to hear about something like this. It spoke directly to the longing in my heart. I knew this was a personal invitation that I was meant to go. I held onto the Miraculous Medal they gave me and prayed I would be able to visit.

Not long after, my mom also felt a strong desire to go. We looked into pilgrimages and there was one going in June. Although it was already April, we still hadn't booked because my parents were concerned about our traveling to a country that was so recently in turmoil. There were still live land mines there. My mom decided to call the tour guide and share her concerns. Carol, who's lead over 50 tours to Medjugorje, simply said, "I want you to know there's another family with two young adults going on this pilgrimage and that usually doesn't happen, so it might be good for your daughter." This was enough for us to realize we were meant to go, despite the perceived danger. Our flights were booked and the two of us were going to Medjugorje that June.

I broke up with my long-term boyfriend shortly before we left because I felt I needed this time to focus on God. I didn't want anything to distract me from Our Lord. I would be spending my 21st birthday praying instead of drinking. Only Our Lord and Our Lady could arrange such a thing.

On this pilgrimage, I experienced many graces. I went to confession for the first time in years. It would have been hard not to go because there are more than 50 confessionals in every language imaginable, offered every day for many hours. It is difficult to describe Medjugorje because the peace and love there transcends human words. The best way I can describe it is that it's heavenly. It feels like a little bit of heaven on earth. Things that I thought were so important back home like fashion, trends, technology, and going out, all had little value there. In Medjugorje, my heart was turned toward heavenly things. I was seeking a deeper relationship with Jesus and Mary. I realized that this was truly living. Not knowing what I wanted to do once I graduated with a degree in graphic design, integrated media and marketing, I remember telling Our Lady, *I just want to work for you. I'll do anything for you!* I took everything in. I wanted to live the five stones: Holy Mass, daily rosary, monthly confession, fasting Wednesdays and Fridays, and reading Scripture daily.

I returned home with resolutions and a strong desire to go back to Medjugorje. I went back the following summer with my friend, Christina, one of the young adults whom I met on the first trip. She was filming a documentary, *Queen of Peace*, and I went as a friend to help with interviews and capture different shots. We were there for the Youth Festival with thousands of other young people. It was truly a blessed time. Medjugorje had found a special place in my heart.

When I returned to the U.S. from my second trip, I entered into full battle. I was living between two worlds. I wanted and desired prayer and holiness, and yet I was surrounded by the party life. There's a Scripture passage from Luke that says, "When an unclean spirit goes out of someone, it roams through arid regions searching for rest but, finding none, it says, 'I shall return to my home from which I came.' But upon returning, it finds it swept clean and put in order. Then it goes and brings back seven other spirits more wicked than itself who move in and dwell there, and the last condition of that person is worse than the first" (Luke 11:24-26). This describes me exactly as I was during that time. I was swept clean, yet I opened the door to drinking again, and I became worse. This time drinking led to other destructive behaviors. I was living two lives again. I should note that even though I had been to confession in Medjugorje and again when I returned, I still had not confessed my involvement with the occult because I didn't know it was a sin. God knew I'd need a very special blessing for that.

In December of 2011, I went to an event at the Cathedral of the Holy Cross and I heard a nun speak about confession. Her name was Mother Olga Yaqob, and while I was listening to her I knew I had to meet her. I had come to a point in my life that I needed to surrender to God. I was tired of living as I was. For instance, one weekend I was too hung over to go to an Ignatian retreat that I had registered (and paid!) for. I knew she could help me.

In meeting with Mother Olga, I was immediately attracted to religious life. Prayer, Mass, Adoration, work, formation, simplicity, and schedule were all things my unholy self longed for. I joined the Daughters of Mary of Nazareth for the trip to Washington DC for the March for Life and I assimilated fast. I was quickly falling in love with everything about religious life, even wearing plain black shoes because it didn't matter anymore. I remember cleaning and clearing out my clothes and shoes. I gave away a pair of nearly new Ugg boots and was joyful about it. I told God, *I give it all to you. I'll do anything for you.* I knew he knew best, and I trusted in his way. He was giving me freedom. During this six month period of time, I was stripped of many worldly possessions, stripped of myself, and stripped of unhealthy friendships. I received a voicemail late one night from someone whom I thought was my friend saying, "How can you do this! You are crazy! What's all this God stuff? This isn't you! You don't know what you're doing." It was painful, but I knew God was taking away those unhealthy friendships. I also recognized how many people I needed to ask for forgiveness. I began that process slowly, especially with my family and then my friends. I think my brother was most moved by my apology when I told him how sorry I was for being a bad influence. When we were younger, he looked up to me and I realized how I crushed him. My brother saw everything I went through, and it must have been so hard for him. I still pray in reparation for the pain I caused my family.

A true turning point in my life was during the community's annual Lenten retreat. It was led by Msgr. John Esseff. This very holy priest was St. Mother Teresa's spiritual director. He was also prayed over by St. Padre Pio. Msgr. Esseff has a very beautiful gift like St. Pio did in the confessional. We spent two days preparing for our confessions. The talks he gave were incredibly wise. He said that only the Holy Spirit could reveal our sins to us. He told us to ask the Holy Spirit what our sins were. What was keeping us from God? Where was the pus in our souls? He invited us to look back over our lives for tendencies that we might have had as a child that evolved into sins.

I was praying before the tabernacle asking the Holy Spirit to tell me my sins. He spoke to me in the silence of my heart and reminded me of one thing, then another and another. All these things about the occult came up. I asked him, What is all this? What is this sin? The answer was very clear: I was interested in the works of the devil. I broke down and cried and cried and cried. I remember thinking, *Me? That's what I've been dealing with all these years?* I continued to cry in my contrition, sorrow, shame, and guilt.

Our confessions were the next day, and I will share with you that it was the worst night of my life. I wanted to leave the retreat. I wanted to deny it all. My skin was literally crawling and I couldn't settle my mind. Looking back, I see that this was the evil one's attempt to keep me in my sins because he knew that the next morning I would confess them, and then be forgiven and freed. I begged the Blessed Mother to stay with me. I remember lying in bed and holding out my hand into the dark room saying, "Mother Mary, I need you to hold my hand all night. You cannot leave my bedside, please. I need you." And she did. She brought me peace and comforted me so I would stay.

The next morning, I prayed that I would be the first to go to confession. I could NOT wait. Mother Olga drafted the order and posted it. I was first.

It was the most beautiful confession of my life. When I finished, Msgr. Esseff asked me, "Look at Jesus in your heart, what do you see?" I expected to see Our Lord looking at me with disappointment and judgment, but no. This image is what I saw:

Jesus was looking at me with love, compassion and mercy. I thought, *He loves me so much!* Msgr. Esseff then asked if I needed a hug. I said, "How did you know?" I also received an Anointing of the Sick and I had profound peace. I was finally back in the shepherd's fold.

At the same time, I still couldn't believe what I had confessed. I remember reflecting, *I don't think I'll ever be able to share this with anyone.* And here I am writing about it. I can describe it now because Jesus came into this very dark part of me and replaced it with his light. By his wounds we are healed. Jesus said, "Those who are healthy do not need a physician, but the sick do. I have not come to call the righteous to repentance but sinners" (Luke 5:31-32). Lord, thank you for calling me to repentance and restoring me to life.

I officially entered Mother Olga's community, the Daughters of Mary of Nazareth, on Easter Sunday 2012. As Mother Olga reflected, this was my resurrection. The Lord had given me new life. In the following days, I found myself asking God if this was truly my vocation. Growing up, I had always pictured myself as a wife and mother, and yet I was willing to surrender it all to God. Whatever he wanted for me was what I wanted. My parents had originally been supportive of my discernment about religious life, but toward the end, they didn't think it was a good fit for me.

I should point out that after having disobeyed and disrespected my parents for a number of years, I now wanted to respect them and not cause them any more pain. Their questioning certainly played into my decision to leave the community after about six months. It wasn't easy. I left the Daughters of Mary of Nazareth somewhat relieved that the relationship with my parents was restored, yet I was unsure of where God was calling me next. I had peace that my vocation was to be a wife and mother. Throughout this time in the community, I thought I was pursuing religious life for God, but it was the opposite. He was doing it for me. This was the greatest blessing. My relationship with Jesus grew so deep and I experienced a new love during this time as well — a love for the Catholic Church. I left the community knowing God used this time to heal me in many ways and to teach me how to be a true follower of Christ.

God has a sense of humor because I met a man, Christian, a few months after I left the community. Mind you, I was not looking to date or to be in a relationship. I was spending my free time in Adoration and keeping my focus on Jesus. After a young adult Mass, I was introduced to Christian and I was immediately attracted to his constant joy and peace. He reminded me so much of Our Lord — steady, unchanging, a rock. We began dating a few months later, and all the while I was asking the Lord, *Is this what you want?* The confirmations and consolations kept coming. Our dating was beautiful, fun and very blessed. We had met at St. Leonard's in the North End of Boston, and that's also where we were engaged. We grew in our love of God and one another. We would meet for 7 a.m. Mass during the week and then scurry off to our jobs. We spent time together in Adoration and visited the National Shrine of Divine Mercy in Stockbridge, MA. We laughed while marking each other in pick-up soccer and trekked across Boston in the snow.

At this point, I had started working for a Catholic apostolate, *Live the Fast*, a nonprofit that promoted prayer and fasting. It was founded by Andrew LaVallee after his profound "reconversion" in Medjugorje. It turned out that we were both there for the first time, at the same time, in June 2010, but we didn't know each other. My prayer had been answered. I was working for Our Lady of Medjugorje. It was the perfect combination of my skill set, education and faith. Again, only God could have arranged it. Our Lady had me using graphic design to make flyers, business cards, prayer cards etc., and filming videos of different priests and doctors talking about fasting. I wrote bi-weekly email reminders for the Live the Fast community offering words of encouragement to fast. The community prayed and fasted for submitted prayer intentions and we witnessed multiple answered prayers, such as a six-year-old girl being healed of cancer.

Holy Mass was part of my lunch break and a Divine Mercy Chaplet walk at three o'clock was included in my workday, along with a rosary in the morning. I saw how I could take what I had learned in the religious community and apply it to my daily life. God gave me the grace to structure my day around prayer. I remember reflecting often, *I can't believe this is my job.*

In the first draft of this book Christian hadn't been to Medjugorje, but on October 1, 2017 he made his way there. He says that while he didn't experience a miracle like the sun spinning, he came back loving to pray. Our Lady also commissioned him for a project that is still unfolding. We continue to be amazed how God is at work in our life. Our wedding was on October 4, 2013 — the Feast of St. Francis. We chose this date as a reminder to serve, give to the poor, and have an open heart and home. We also took a few minutes right after we exchanged vows and rings to consecrate our marriage to Our Lady.

In the four and a half years we've been married, we've been blessed to grow deeper in our faith and love under Our Lady's mantle. We welcomed our first daughter, Mariella Therese, in August 2014 and our second daughter, Zelie Anne, in August 2016. Every day we pray to grow in holiness and to become the spouses and parents God created us to be. We have also been stretched and tried in many ways, which has been challenging as a young married couple and family. We faced unemployment for Christian for many months, moving twice in one year, and also the sudden passing of Christian's father. We have been able to relate well to the Holy Family's unexpected situations, such as the flight into Egypt during their early family life.

So here we are today. Having been through everything I have in search of peace, I can tell you that I have found the source — the King of Peace himself, Jesus Christ. My hope rests in God's infinite mercy and I joyfully meditate on meeting him face to face, when he will say to me, "Well done, good and faithful servant . . . Come, share your master's joy" (Matthew 25:23).

Before you begin, I have a quick practical note about reading this book. Thanks to a dear friend, Miriam, who suggested making this book ready for small faith-sharing groups. After first reading it by herself, Miriam felt inspired to gather a small group together once a month to discuss and to support one another putting each chapter into practice. With that said, at the end of each chapter, you'll find questions for personal reflection, questions for small group discussion, and action items.

It is my prayer that you will find one of the following chapters helpful on your path to answer Our Lady's call to become a living Gospel. By learning and following Our Lady's five stones of prayer, fasting, Confession, Holy Mass and reading Scripture, your heart will be opened for God's plan for you. "For I know well the plans I have in mind for you—oracle of the LORD—plans for your welfare and not for woe, so as to give you a future of hope" (Jeremiah 29:11).

May the Lord bless you and keep you, and may Our Lady wrap her mantle around you.

All for the glory and praise of God, now and forever,
Darcie Nielsen

Photos

Maximilian and I (1996)

Drinking water at Lourdes (1992)

My First Communion (1997)

High School Graduation (2007)

Night out (2011)

Anointing by Msgr. Esseff (2012)

Below: Family after entering community (2012)

Working at Live the Fast (2013)

Medjugorje (2012)

Our wedding (2013) Photo Credit: George Martell

Enthronement of the Sacred Heart in our home (2013)

Mother Olga bringing our first child, Mariella, to Jesus in the Blessed Sacrament (2014)

Thanksgiving with the family (2017)

Let's not forget

Chapter 2

Let's not forget. Even though we've embraced the faith, we are still going to struggle. We are not immune to suffering, trials or death. We are still human beings corrupted by original sin. But now we accept that we are children of God. That is why Jesus prayed for us, "I do not ask that you take them out of the world but that you keep them from the evil one" (John 17:15). That is also why he taught us the Our Father: "... lead us not into temptation, but deliver us from evil." We are prone to fall into temptation, which then leads to sin.

Heaven is rejoicing with us, which also means hell is furious. We were once batting for the other team and bringing others with us. The evil one pretty much left us alone because we were making bad decisions on our own. We weren't a threat to him and any time we started to drift to God and holiness, he'd find a way to lure us back.

It's different now. We've rejected Satan. (Though he doesn't deserve a capital "s.") We've repented. We're in full communion with God. We're on our way to heaven and to becoming a saint. And we're bringing as many people with us as possible. So, the evil one is furious. Not only is he angry, he's also resentful. He still thinks he has a chance. Ha! We are God's now, and with his grace, he will lead us through all difficulties. Jesus tells us, "In the world you will have trouble, but take courage, I have conquered the world" (John 16:33).

St. Paul helps us live our new life, "Brothers and sisters: You were once in darkness, but now you are light in the Lord. Live as children of light, for light produces every kind of goodness and righteousness and truth.

Try to learn what is pleasing to the Lord. Take no part in the fruitless works of darkness; the things done by them in secret; but everything exposed by the light becomes visible, for everything that becomes visible is light. Therefore, it says: 'Awake, O sleeper, and arise from the dead, and Christ will give you light' " (Ephesians 5:8-14).

Start here

Chapter 3

Start here, with confession.

Most pilgrims go to confession in Medjugorje. It'd be hard not to. When you walk along the side of St. James Church and see the lines for confession in all different languages, it makes you want to be a part of it. There's a sense that something very powerful and beautiful is going on. I remember thinking, *Wow, these people look so happy after and even during confession. I want to experience that too.* I saw how lovingly the priests listened to people share their sins, nodding along, asking questions and finally giving absolution. It was the opposite of what I had expected. I had built up confession in my head to be this horrible, sad, shameful experience. And for the first time in my life, I saw that the focus of confession wasn't on one's shame and guilt, but rather on God bestowing his mercy. It was a sacrament of love! When we're coming back to God, we need to begin with this encounter of love. We need to start with confession.

As Our Lady said in her July 2, 2007 message, "Dear children! In the great love of God, I come to you today to lead you on the way of humility and meekness. The first station on that way, my children, is confession. Reject your arrogance and kneel down before my Son. Comprehend, my children, that you have nothing and you can do nothing. The only thing that is yours and what you possess is sin. Be cleansed and accept meekness and humility. My Son could have won with strength, but he chose meekness, humility and love. Follow my Son and give me your hands so that, together, we may climb the mountain and win. Thank you." So let's take Our Lady at her word and begin with confession.

In Medjugorje, that place of prayer and holiness, the ugliness of our sinfulness comes to the surface to be purified. We start to understand our nothingness. We realize our pride. We are able to have a deep examination of conscience and knowledge of what we need to confess — even if it was something 10, 20, or 30 years ago. In fact, we learn that there's a lot we need to confess, and that this knowledge often leads us to a "general" or "life" confession, as it's called. This confession encompasses every mortal sin from the age of reason (beginning at 7 or 8 years old) until the present day, whether confessed before or not. If you've had this experience, then you can skip ahead to the next section on *Attending Confession Regularly*. But if you're like me and didn't make your life confession in Medjugorje (or yet), then read on!

Making a life confession

The fact that you're reading this section means your life confession is already on your heart. Maybe you're at a point when you're preparing for your monthly confession and past sins come up that you think you confessed before, but can't remember. Or maybe you haven't been to confession in years. Whatever the case may be, the promptings you have for a life confession are from the Holy Spirit.

It was only recently that I made my life confession - on December 8, 2015. What a blessing! I wish I had gone sooner. To be honest, it was my pride and stubbornness that kept me from going. I felt I had come so far and I was disgusted with who I once was. There was a part of me that didn't want to think about all my sins again, especially because I confessed many of them before. It was overwhelming how much I had offended God, and to put it all out there at once was intimidating. God was so patient with me, as he is with each one of us. He always has the best timing, and perhaps my seemingly "delayed" life confession gave me the grace to write now about it's importance. St. Josemaria recommended doing a yearly general confession, mentioning the sins of the past year. Annual retreats are a good time.

I first heard about life confession from Andy LaVallee when I worked at *Live the Fast*. Andy made his life confession in Medjugorje and, as he says, three hours later he was a new man. Hearing him talk about it made me want to go, but then I assumed my confession with Msgr. Esseff counted. Maybe you've had a similar situation. You've been growing in the faith and have had some very contrite and beautiful confessions, but there hasn't been that life confession that your heart desires. Thankfully, St. Francis de Sales wrote about the value of starting with a general confession too:

> "But, furthermore, a general confession forces us to a clearer self-knowledge, kindles a wholesome shame for our past life, and rouses gratitude for God's Mercy, which has so long waited patiently for us;–it comforts the heart, refreshes the spirit, excites good resolutions, affords opportunity to our spiritual Father for giving the most suitable advice, and opens our hearts so as to make future confessions more effectual. Therefore I cannot enter into the subject of a general change of life and entire turning to God, by means of a devout life, without urging upon you to begin with a general confession."[1]

Preparing for my life confession was amazing. It took a couple hours over the course of three days. Yes, I needed that time to recall my past sins specifically in their nature, degree, and frequency; I did not want to leave anything out. I wrote it all down. I wanted to confess everything and be done with it, once and for all. Afterwards, I no longer hesitated. God in his mercy does not keep tabs, so why should I? He forgave me, allowing me to forgive myself. If you're being weighed down by your past and the mistakes you made, seek freedom in the life confession. As Jesus told St. Faustina, "Let no soul fear to approach Me, even though its sins be as scarlet."[2]

---

[1] St. Francis de Sales, Introduction to the Devout Life (New York: Catholic Way Publishing, 2015), Chapter Six.

[2] Saint Faustina, Diary of Saint Maria Faustina Kowalska: Divine Mercy in My Soul (Stockbridge, MA: Marian Press, 2005), 286.

Maybe you haven't been to confession in years. Maybe you're confused about what constitutes a sin, never mind a mortal or venial sin. Maybe you're a little intimidated by the thought of confession, and all the more by a life confession. Maybe you can't remember how confession goes. "Do I start or does the priest?" You might even think that you're the worst sinner in the world and that your confession will absolutely shock the priest.

You're in the right place. What you're feeling is completely normal. We can learn from our Holy Father, Pope Francis. In an interview shortly after becoming Pope, he was asked who he is. His answer? "I am a sinner. This is the most accurate definition. It is not a figure of speech, a literary genre. I am a sinner."[3] We are all sinners — "The church is not a museum for saints but a hospital for sinners" (St. Augustine of Hippo).

As for thinking you'll shock the priest with your sins — guess what? They have heard it all. I'll never forget what an elderly priest once said about confession in encouraging us to go. First, they have heard it all. Nothing is a surprise. Second, they don't remember what you said in confession. They really don't. They hear hundreds of confessions a month. Third, they are bound by a vow not to share what was said in confession. For example, if you've robbed someone and you mention this in confession, the priest cannot report you. Even if the police were to question him, he could not share what you said in the confessional. That's how powerful the seal of the confessional is.

I think it's important to note that withholding a sin in confession is a sin, a grave sin. If that's something on your conscience, bring it to the light. Jesus already knows and he wants to forgive you. Jesus tells us, "There will be more joy in heaven over one sinner who repents than over ninety-nine righteous people who have no need of repentance" (Luke 15:7). We bring joy to heaven by going to confession.

---

[3] Stephen Bullivant, "I am a Sinner." America Magazine. Last modified 25 September, 2013. <http://americamagazine.org/issue/%E2%80%98i-am-sinner%E2%80%99>

So how do we prepare for this life confession?

You know the answer: prayer. Ask the Holy Spirit to enlighten you and to give you humility. But first, be aware that you might not like what he will reveal to you. Keep in mind that he's helping you. Ask him, "What sins in my life are keeping me from God?" "What do I need to confess?" "What sins do I have that I've been ignoring?" Take a few moments to be silent and listen. There will most likely be something that you'll want to dismiss right away. "Me? There's no way. I'm not like that" might be your self-talk, but this is when it's so important to be humble, and to accept what the Holy Spirit is revealing to you. Ask the Holy Spirit what tendencies you've had since childhood. This may give you a good indication of how those same tendencies might be manifesting themselves as sins in your adult life. Were you jealous when your classmate received an honor and you didn't? Were you particularly curious about kissing and everything that went along with it? Were you interested in horoscopes? Did you get excited when you got away with lying to your parents? We often don't take the time to look back at ourselves as children, but once we do, especially in the light of preparing for confession, we recognize tendencies that evolved into sins as we grew older. Let us also pray to the Blessed Mother and our guardian angels to help us prepare for this life confession.

Now is when we need a solid examination of conscience. A helpful resource is the website, www.thelightisonforyou.org. Each commandment has questions for you to answer. Write down your sins. Take each one slowly. It is important to be specific. For example, if you missed Sunday Mass for a period of time, it's not enough to say, "I missed Sunday Mass a bunch of times." Be specific: "I missed Sunday Mass for 12 years." Don't be surprised if you broke all the commandments. There may be many tears in this process as we see how much we've offended God and recognize the full extent of our sinfulness. The importance of the life confession is that you get everything out and receive God's healing mercy.

Start praying for the priest who will hear your life confession — not because you don't want him to fall over, but so that he is guided by the

Holy Spirit to counsel you. Perhaps you want to go to a priest you've never seen and never will again. Or maybe you want this to be the start of having a regular confessor. For example, I went to a priest in a religious order (instead of diocesan) for my life confession, which you might also prefer.

All I can say is that when I finished confessing, the priest was quiet for a moment. For a second I thought he might have left! But then he said with a smile in his voice, "is that everything?" It put me right at ease and I understood that Jesus in his infinity saw my sins as a drop in the ocean. When Jesus was on the cross he knew what sins we'd commit and he still died for us. He paid the price so we might live. Give him and all of heaven great joy and go for that life confession.

Attending confession regularly

So now we can delve into regular confession (as in, confession which we attend regularly). Building upon your life confession, regular confession will continue to change your life.

No matter how many times I've been, my hands still get clammy and my heart races while waiting in line. You're probably like me and have a love-hate relationship with confession. You love it because you encounter Jesus and receive mercy and pardon for your sins, but hate it because you have to say your sins out loud to a priest. It's humbling. And humility is always where we need to start, again and again. Our Lady said in part of her November 25, 1998 message, "May holy confession be the first act of conversion for you and then, dear children, decide for holiness." Every time we go to confession, we decide for holiness.

If there's a sin you've been struggling with for a long time, bring it to confession. Even if you just went last week or yesterday. Bring that sin to confession as many times as needed. God doesn't tire of giving his Mercy (he's infinite, remember?), though we may tire of asking for it. Don't give up. The problem with our sins is that we like them. They developed out of bad habits, which means they've been around for a while and we're comfortable with them. Even though there's a part of us that knows they're bad, this familiarity helps us rationalize our way into believing that they're innocuous. It's time to get uncomfortable. Have you ever seen a baby learning to walk? For months they've been crawling around on the ground. They see adults doing all sorts of things above them and realize there's a whole new world. Babies start to pull themselves up on anything they can, but they fall often because their feet aren't coordinated. They even twist their ankles sometimes. We are like these babies in our spiritual journey. Learning to walk is awkward and uncomfortable. And just like babies, we will often fall, but we must keep trying to walk or else we'll never be able to explore the new world. We'll never be able to run. As long as we like our sins, we'll keep doing them. You turn a corner when you start to hate your sins. This comes from a greater love for God because you'll naturally love what he loves and hate what he hates (sin). Our Lady encourages us in her March 25, 2014 message, "Dear children! I am calling you anew: begin the battle against sin as in the first days, go to and decide for holiness…"

Sin is best described as anything that is keeping you from loving God and accepting his love. The measure of holiness is love. If we look to the saints, we can see that they lived in love. We are called to this same love. Our perfection is not in being "sin-free," but rather in the purity and intensity of our love, and in getting up again and again when we fall.

We are called to love each day and at each moment of our lives; this is the goal. If we sincerely ask ourselves if we're living this truth, we can see how often we fall short over the course of just one day. Scripture tells us that the just man falls seven times a day. So that's why we need to go to confession regularly, because things, people, ideas and situations disturb the purity and the intensity of our love and peace.

Here's the hard truth: Because of original sin, we have inherited this tendency to sin. We are sinners. It's difficult to accept because we want to be perfect for God. We want to be holy and we want to do everything to bring about his kingdom. Consider, then, that the kingdom is our heart, and that it is within our hearts that God wants us to apply ourselves and to wage the battle against sin. We might think, "Ugh, but I want to be a missionary."

Regular confession gives us the opportunity to check in with the Divine Doctor. We're able to bring him all our pains, worries, and failures, and he transforms them into glory. Part of experiencing reconversion (or conversion) is placing your past into God's mercy and accepting it. Your past made you who you are today. God in his goodness took what you messed up and made it into something beautiful. And guess what? That happens every time we go to confession.

Here's something to think about. When Jesus appeared to his disciples after the Resurrection, he still had his wounds. St. Thomas (a favorite) said that he would not believe Jesus had visited them until he put his finger in Jesus' side. Shortly thereafter, Jesus appeared again and told St. Thomas to do so. The wounds of the crucified Jesus made him who he is. If he didn't have the nail marks in his hands and feet, and the wound from where the spear pierced his side, how would we recognize him? Perhaps the same is true for us. When we die, our "wounds" won't just disappear, because they made us who we are. But they will be glorified, as were Jesus' five holy wounds.

This is why humility is so important when it comes to our spiritual life. In spite of all our sins and wickedness, we are still loved and shown mercy. Regular confession helps us grow in humility. We need it because to recognize our faults and to ask forgiveness is the antithesis of pride, which is considered the root of all sin. Know, too, that the evil one doesn't want you on this path. He doesn't want you going to confession regularly and he will try to take you off course. Commit to a monthly confession. I have often found that having confession on my calendar helps me better prepare and even to look forward to it. If you're going through a difficult time or struggling in your personal life, don't be afraid to go more often. It will give you the strength to persevere through the suffering. Especially because our wickedness tends to come out more readily when we're hurting, whether physically, spiritually or emotionally. It's good to be childlike in this matter. Don't try to self-help or WebMD it — get to the Divine Doctor. It's also important to note that certain issues do need to be further explored with the help of a psychologist or another specialist. After all, God gave us science, too.

One time, a priest in confession did refer me to a psychologist. So I made an appointment and went. I was amazed because I realized I was trying to use confession as a mediator in a certain relationship. Instead of talking to that person about what was going on, I would let myself get frustrated and angry, not say anything, and then bring it to confession. Maybe this sounds familiar to you. It sounds like a no-brainer, but I learned that I needed to talk to the person and express that what they were doing was affecting me in a negative way. After talking with them, the strain in our relationship was lifted and the sacrament of confession was restored to its rightful place.

I'm still learning how to go to confession and I think that's something we'll always be working on. Another time, I went to confession because I had been doing some spiritual reading and I recognized something the author described as being in myself — falling short of loving God wholeheartedly. The priest asked me, "So what's the sin in this?" I laughed and said, "I don't know!" He suggested that this was something I was prompted to pray with, to desire more and to grow in. I learned that this was something for spiritual direction, not confession.

Our Lady asks us to go to confession once a month, as she said in part of her message of August 6, 1982, "Monthly confession will be a remedy for the Church in the West." Stick with that guideline unless you've committed a mortal sin, and then go sooner of course. We may also find as we continue on our spiritual journey that we want to go twice a month or even every week as St. Josemaria also suggested for those who really wanted to grow in the spiritual life. That's beautiful too. The more we love God, the more we become aware of sinfulness in us and around us.

I'd like to end with a story that I heard from a priest not too long ago. He said he was waiting in line at a store and a man came up to him with tears in his eyes and voice cracking said, "Tell me, why does my six-year-old daughter have cancer? Why?" The priest took a moment and responded, "Because of my sin." The man was taken aback. The priest went on, "That's the ugliness and hurt of sin. We do not know how and where its effects will be, and since we are all connected, our sins affect one another." I will never forget this, and I often recall this story before confession. It inspires me to make my confession the best I can because it's not just about me. It makes me want to live in a way that all my choices and my life bring blessings to the world and to the Body of Christ.

"Whoever is in Christ is a new creation: the old things have passed away; behold, new things have come. And all this is from God, who has reconciled us to himself through Christ and given us the ministry of reconciliation ..." (2 Corinthians 5:17).

Questions for Your Personal Reflection
1. What is keeping me from loving God?
2. How can I modify my schedule to fit in regular confession?
3. What am I afraid of?
4. What specifically will I do differently in preparing for my next confession?

Questions for Small Group Discussion
1. Have you noticed a trend in your sins? What impact has that had on your spiritual life?
2. How are you handling doubts and nerves in preparing for confession, especially if doing a life confession?
3. What are some practical strategies to make enough time to prepare?

Action Item
Prepare for life confession, make appointment and do it.

Just because you've changed...

Chapter 4

The thing about conversion is that it happens at different times for different people. While you wish everyone you knew went to Medjugorje with you, they didn't. Your family and friends have become used to your being a certain way. So when you start acting, talking and doing new things in living the Gospel, they often won't know how to respond. The Gospel is radical, and when we start living radically, it makes others uncomfortable. They might have a lot of questions and you might not have all the answers. They might even think you have lost it. Be aware that well-meaning friends and family will talk with you and act with you as if nothing has changed. They might pull you into conversations and ways of thinking with which you once agreed, but now you see differently and may disagree with them.

These relationships are probably the hardest to navigate as you live your new life after returning from Medjugorje. Be prepared to be left out and not invited to certain things anymore. But remember, it is our call to keep loving and forgiving. It can be hard when we want to be bitter, but the Gospel calls us to love, especially those who persecute us, which could end up being those who are closest. You might hear, "I know you! The way you're living isn't you. I know who you really are." This can get you to question yourself, but remember who really knows you the best: God, your father in heaven. He wants your ultimate happiness and he wants you to come to heaven. God also does some pruning of unhealthy and "surface" relationships and thus some might naturally dissolve. It can be painful, but trust that new sprouts will grow with new friendships. During this time, the evil one will also try to isolate you. He will try to convince you that you're a loner and that no one else is living this way. He will invite you to question your whole conversion, your faith and even God. Isolation for us humans is dangerous. Be at peace. This is why this chapter is about finding faith-filled friends and community.

Begin at your Catholic Church. Start going to a regular Mass and start looking for people who share Christ's joy and who are trying to live the Gospel. It can be hard because you could go to Mass and leave without anyone acknowledging you. For those introverts reading, this might be a challenge, but you must put yourself out there. Introduce yourself. You might be surprised how warm and welcoming we Catholics are, once you break the ice. If you're a young adult like I was, join a young adult group. No matter what age you are, participate in something in the Church. Maybe it's a Bible study, chaplain ministry, soup kitchen, religious education teacher, volunteer, etc. Look in the bulletin or on the website and find something. In this way, you will start to meet people. Then, those people will introduce you to new people. If you make the commitment to start finding faith-filled friends and a community, God will provide. It might take perseverance and time, but God will start putting people in your life. My husband said that when he joined a young adult group, he went every week, but every week he had to re-introduce himself to the same people. The temptation was to stop going, but he resolved to continue. He said, "God will reward me in my commitment." It was through that group that we met through a mutual friend…

These new faith-filled friends and community will help you live your conversion. They will give you support, and often you will meet someone who has experience in exactly what you're going through. When I had first thought about religious life and I hadn't shared it with anyone but The Lord, I was at a cookout (through someone I met at church, I might add). I got to talking with Michael and wouldn't you know, he's a seminarian. He's studying to be a priest. I knew this was a gift from God, and I shared with him that I felt called to discern religious life. The conversation was absolutely blessed, and I remember writing down books he recommended. My husband and I are still friends with him to this day. What's important to note about being part of a new community and friends is that it requires us to open up. Now I'm not saying, go and trust everyone you meet with your life, but to have an openness of heart. We are called to be authentic and true in all of our relationships. The setting of a faith community gives us the opportunity to be who we really are and hopefully meet and see others as they really are. True friendships start to form and a trust is built that might not have been present in former relationships.

If there's someone who was there for a big part of your conversion or traveled with you to Medjugorje, then stay in touch—even if it's an occasional email or phone call. That person can pray for you, but more importantly, just speaking with them reignites the fire for The Lord. For me, these people are Christina and Carol. They probably don't even know it! Every time I see them, I am reminded of what Our Lady and Jesus did for me and I'm moved to deeper gratitude. I'm encouraged and inspired to keep growing in faith. We are all pilgrims together on the journey to our homeland, heaven. We need one another.

Another trap from the evil one is to convince us that we don't need anyone, to think that we're stronger when we're in control and independent. We think that when we let someone in, we're being vulnerable and that we'll get hurt or be judged. We only need to look to Jesus' example and see how he shared his most intimate teachings with the disciples. We need to share with one another and listen to one another. This is one of the greatest gifts of a faith community. When you start spending time together on a regular basis, you start to learn new things about the faith. Maybe you're invited to a retreat or to visit a shrine. When you're strengthened by others in living the faith, you have more confidence in dealing with those well-intentioned loved ones and friends who might be challenging you in your new way of living.

It's important to know too that Satan will still be trying to get you off course. Remember that he was an angel of light, so sometimes he will use his light to attract us but it's a trap. How do we know when this is happening? A great example I have is when I was looking to get involved in a faith community. I was hoping for some sort of Bible study. It had been on my heart to learn more and study the Word of God. I was stopped on the street in Boston by a young woman who said, "Would you like to join a Bible study?" I remember thinking, *Come on! This must be from God.* They told me the meeting place and time later that week. It wasn't at a Catholic church, but I thought, *Well, I've heard that other denominations are better versed in the Bible so it'll be fine.* When I got there with four others, it started off great, but then it took a turn for the worse. All of a sudden I'm being asked, "so who's the female version of God?" Then they go into all this crazy theology. I closed my Bible and simply, said, "what you're saying isn't the truth," and I left. Thankfully there was a Catholic chapel around the corner and I nearly ran there. I thanked God for showing me the truth and giving me the courage to leave. When I left the chapel 15 minutes later, I circled back to see if they were still there because I thought, *if this was a true Bible study, then they would still be studying regardless if I left.* But they were not. It hit me then that I was a target. Satan was still after me. (Just a note, this organization is classified as a cult and is called Eastern Lightning, so stay away.)

So the lesson is: for now, stay in the Catholic faith. This goes for Bible studies, prayer groups and spiritual reading. We're babies on our journey of faith, and we need to be close to Mother church so as to be nourished by the truth. Maybe later on in our journey, God will put us in places to give witness and engage in apologetics, and we'll have had the training to do it. Until then, don't stray.

I'd like to share one more example of the evil one using "light" to attract us. As the Psalmist says, "Evil's flattering light disguises his wickedness, so that he does not hate it." (Psalm 35 - the sinner's wickedness; God's goodness.) Once I had found myself in a Catholic Bible study, thanks be to God. A young man who attended belonged to the Church of Christ, Scientist, commonly known as Christian Science. At the end of one of the discussions, he approached me about doing freelance graphic design work for the local Christian Science Center. (During the introductions we usually shared our line of work.) I remember thinking, *What's the risk? I know the fullness of truth is in the Catholic faith. An extra job is good. Maybe I could even evangelize this young man.* As I began exploring the opportunity and actually visited the Christian Science Center, it did not settle well in my heart. I would essentially be working for another faith. I'd be helping them advance their mission and cause, which is different than the Catholic faith. As a baptized Catholic, I am called to proclaim the Gospel — the truth. It seemed a little funny to be spending lots of time at a Christian Science Center instead of a Catholic church, which has the true presence of Jesus in the Blessed Sacrament, right? I talked to some faith-filled friends about it, and they were in agreement. I saw the truth and did not accept the freelance work. It goes to show that once I was in a Catholic Bible study, the evil one was still trying to get me off course.

We need the support of faith-filled friends and community. Be aware that it is when you are first getting started that there will be the most distractions. The evil one does not want you to have this support because he knows how powerful community is. We see it in the early Christians, throughout Church history and today. Persevere in finding that community and pray to the Lord to help you.

"For where two or three are gathered together in my name, there am I in the midst of them" (Jesus in Matthew 18:20).

Questions for Your Personal Reflection
1. How am I going to get involved in the faith community?
2. What steps will I take to be better prepared while maintaining peace for those difficult conversations?
3. Am I being called to start something at my church? A Bible study? Rosary group?

Questions for Small Group Discussion

1. Is there a faith-related group that I'm part of that isn't settling well in my heart? (Hopefully not this one!) Why not?

2. What are some ways to start praying in my family?

3. Moving forward, how will I discern God's will about joining a prayer group, Bible study, faith-sharing, etc.?

Action Item

Join or start a faith-based group at your parish.

Stuff, stuff and more stuff

Chapter 5

From the title of this chapter, you can probably guess what it is all about. It's time to get rid of *stuff*. You might be thinking, what does this have to do with our conversion journey? Just as you had a life confession to get rid of all the emotional baggage, it's time to get rid of the physical baggage. And we all have it. The accumulation of material goods weighs us down. They take up space in our mind and heart. We worry about them — will they get lost or stolen? Do we have enough of them? It seems that the more we have, the more we worry. It's so strange, because we can't take any of our belongings with us when we die. You might have been thinking about this for a while, but haven't had the courage to do it. Well, now is the time to clear out our living space, and that's what this chapter is all about.

Our Lady said in part of her message from April 25, 2000, "You are concerned too much about material things and little about spiritual ones." That is profound. She understands us, that we live in both the material and the spiritual world. She sympathizes with us because she knows how much easier it is for us to focus on the things we can see instead of the things we can't. That is why Our Lady encourages us, "Therefore, little children, do not seek comfort in material things, but rather seek God" (September 25, 1993). When we grow in detachment from our material things, we are better able to focus on God. And one way to start growing in this detachment is to have fewer belongings.

The best place to start is with those clothes, shoes, and other items that you treasured and wore during your days of darkness and sin. They only remind you of your sinfulness anyway, so why keep them around? I can remember looking at a whole section of my closet with my going-out tops that I was now ashamed to have. It was time for them to go. Yes, you might have spent a lot of money on them, but you will find great freedom in not having them anymore. In fact, you might only be keeping them because you spent lots of money on them.

We all have those places in our closets with clothes we don't wear. Most of the time it's because they don't fit. We keep them, though, because we hope to fit into them someday. If you don't fit in them today — right now — get rid of them. They only make you unhappy anyway because you see them and think, "Ugh, I need to lose weight. I need to fit in them again." Then, we have the clothes that we hang onto because there just "might" be that occasion to wear them. You've had them for five years and that occasion hasn't arisen, so it's time to get rid of those too. They'll be out of style by the time the occasion actually comes and you'll want a new style anyway. Why take up the space?

You may have also discovered that in your time away from the faith that you developed some selfishness and a collecting habit. Maybe you have never given to the poor or, if you have, you gave your rattiest clothes that could have really been thrown out. If our hearts are going to be focused on heaven, then we have to be detached from this world. When Jesus asked the disciples to follow him, none of them said, "Can I go back and get my backpack and a change of clothes and my favorite water jug?" No. They followed him with an open trusting heart and with only the clothes on their back. We are called to have that same detachment from our stuff. We must be ready to follow Jesus when He calls us. And we won't hear his call if we're too busy thinking about our stuff and planning how to get more. As Our Lady said, "You get lost easily in material and human things and forget that God is your greatest friend" (February 25, 1992).

To those college-age girls reading this, you can probably relate to this — my shoe collection was off the hook. I had every kind of the shoe for every kind of outfit. All my friends knew who to go to for borrowing shoes. I had so many that I couldn't even store them all in my dorm room. In fact, I kept the different seasons of shoes at my parent's house and switched them out accordingly. I don't even want to know the hundreds of dollars I spent on developing my shoe collection. When it came time for clearing out, I knew the majority of the shoes had to go. I remember giving away a pair of red heels that I loved to a friend, and she even said, "Are you really sure you don't want these anymore?" I wanted to say no, but knew in my heart I wanted to say yes. They became hers.

I should clarify that it doesn't necessarily mean that my personal choices are good for everyone. I discerned in prayer that God was calling me to dwindle down my shoe collection. Did I have more peace afterwards? Absolutely. Did I take better care of the fewer shoes I had? Absolutely. The spirit of poverty is not just having fewer things, but also taking good care of what we have to make it last. A rich person can be poor in spirit, just as a poor person can be attached. It's not a matter of having more or less, but rather our attitude towards what we have.

Oftentimes, we keep things because they were a gift or passed down. As my mom always said (and she had a no-clutter policy for us growing up), "If it doesn't make you happy or if you don't use it, get rid of it." As children, she would put toys and different items we left around the house for more than two days into a bag in the closet. We wouldn't even notice they were missing. Sometimes she would just donate the bag and we had no idea.

Often we don't even realize how much stuff we have. Sometimes we hang onto things because we're afraid that the person who gave it to us would be offended if we got rid of it. Others things have been passed down, such as family heirlooms (that aren't beautiful in any way), and yet we keep them. Take a survey in each room — Do I use this? Does it make me happy? You'll be amazed at how much stuff you don't actually use, and that doesn't make you happy. If you really want to go to town, I recommend the book "The Life-Changing Magic of Tidying Up" by Marie Kondo. While it is secular and I don't agree with her assertion that clothes and objects have "feelings" and that you should talk to them, she does offer a great step-by-step process for cleaning out by category, not location.

Our culture pushes consumerism. It tries to tell us that having more stuff will make us happy, and not just more, but the newest and latest versions. Our Lady warned us of the spirit of consumerism in one of her messages, "In this time when due to the spirit of consumerism one forgets what it means to love and to cherish true values, I invite you again, little children, to put God in first place in your life. Do not let Satan attract you through material things, but, little children, decide for God, who is freedom and love" (March 25, 1996).

At our home, we try to do a clean-out/thinning-out every season (four times a year). It's especially helpful for donating clothes we don't wear for a full season, and also for getting rid of knick-knacks. Sometimes I hesitate and think, "I might just need this one day." I think we all have a tendency to think that. One day, we might just need those individual soufflé dishes (even though we've never made it…). Or one day, I might need three pocket knives. Likewise, one day my good lamp in the living room might bust, so I should keep this spare one just in case. Enough with the "One day…!" We have only one day and that's today. We could die tonight and never use all that extra stuff. Getting rid of stuff helps us live in the present moment. Not to be morbid, but we are all going to die one day. Don't we want to make it really easy for our loved ones to clear out? When we die, we will go and our stuff will stay.

This process took a couple months, but by the end I was a new person. I had a new freedom. It is often said that our living area is a reflection of our souls. When we start working on our souls, we will naturally start working on our living spaces. There's a spiritual tool that can help us in this cleaning out process, and it's fasting.

Now before you roll your eyes and say, "It's only because you worked for *Live the Fast!*" Hear me out. Fasting is one of the five stones Our Lady recommends. It's the one that everyone says, "Oh I do the other four, and so that's four out of five, an 80. That's a B. I'm ok with that." We must remind ourselves again and again that everything Our Lady tells us is for our own good, for our eternal salvation. She is reminding us of the power of fasting. Jesus used this same practice, coupled with prayer, to cast out demons. Our Lady is always pointing us to her Son and to what he did.

The Medjugorje fast is bread and water on Wednesdays and Fridays. This program isn't something we jump into right away. Fasting is a spiritual muscle that takes training and practice, and which gets stronger over time. Always, always check with your doctor first before fasting. I found that a good way to start fasting is by replacing one meal a day on Wednesdays and Fridays with bread and water. Of course, you need the right fasting bread (non-GMO, no additives, preservatives or dough conditioners). No matter how small our efforts may seem at first, the point is to just start fasting.

What about coffee? I love what the visionaries say, "Only if the Blessed Mother doesn't see you!" It's humorous, but it also points to our weakness. Can we really not have coffee for one day? The thing about fasting is that it's meant to detach us from this world. And the more attached we are to the world, the harder it will be to fast. We are afraid of what a new routine without making coffee would be like. We are afraid that we won't have enough nutrients to function. We are, in essence, afraid to die. That is the point. We need to face this fear of death. We need to face the reality that our bodies are deteriorating each day. We need to face the truth that one day we will return to God with nothing but our love and deeds.

I've also heard, "I'm grumpy on fasting days." That's not a reason not to fast! As a fasting priest once said, "It's not that you're grumpy on fast days, but that you're grumpy always and fast days bring it out!" It's true. We are able to suppress our sinful tendencies (perhaps laziness, despair, quick tongue, impatience or anger) when we have full bellies. When we fast, those tendencies seem to come up to the surface instantly. Fasting pops the cork. We face our sinfulness. We realize our bankruptcy. We see that we are incapable of anything good without the grace of God. We need God and that is what fasting teaches us.

Not only do we realize how much we need God, but by fasting we recognize that we are constantly *seeking* God. When we fast, we realize all the little ways we try to cover up that ache for him. We realize how often we turn to everything but Him when we're upset, lonely, sad, angry, joyful, peaceful. That's why fast days are an opportunity to pray more. Moments when you would have turned to coffee for a pick-up, can now be a prayer to the Holy Spirit. Or a moment of starting to lose patience with a toddler is now a plea for grace.

Fasting benefits our body, soul and mind. When I started fasting, it wasn't pretty. I didn't have *Live the Fast* breads so I was finding myself at Panera or Whole Foods on fast days buying a loaf of multigrain. I'd end up eating nearly a whole loaf of bread in one day. This wasn't fasting. This was replacing meals with bread. The point of the bread and water fast is to give us enough energy to keep doing our daily tasks, while experiencing hunger. When we're physically hungry, we are reminded that we are spiritually hungry. We are in solidarity with the poor and those who are perpetually hungry. Fast days are such a freedom because we don't have to think about, plan or make any food. Fasting gives us that break. It takes away the focus on "me, me, and me" and helps us instead to look outwards to others and their needs. More and more scientific studies are coming out with the benefits, especially long-term, of fasting. It is no wonder Scripture and church history are full of fasters.

If you try to make your own fast, it doesn't work. I remember trying to eat just fruit and veggies or no dairy for a "fast" day. We are so good at talking ourselves in and out of things. "Oh I need protein!" would enter my mind and the fast would fail. Bread and water fasting is what the early church lived, and also what Our Lady invites us to live today. That is not to say you can't gradually build up to a bread and water fast, and I've included a flowchart at the end of this chapter to help you.

Fasting is like a reset button for our whole being. It gives us clarity, passions are calmed down and our body has a chance to do repair work and get rid of toxins because it's not spending energy breaking down food. I'll share that I had started to put on weight in high school. A couple pounds here and there. I always thought I was just "five pounds" more than what I wanted to be, but really I'd move up my ideal weight as I gained weight. I tried a bunch of weight loss diets and they'd work for a bit, but then I'd end up gaining more weight because of them. At my heaviest, I was 30 pounds more than what was healthy for my height.

When I started fasting, I didn't expect to lose weight. In many ways, I had given up that effort. What was amazing is that as I fasted, my self-control and self-discipline were sharpened. I also found my fast carrying over to non-fast days. I simply wouldn't have enough room to have that extra portion or snack. My stomach had shrunk. Slowly and surely, the weight started to come off. I didn't even notice until I saw how baggy my clothes were. I was focused so much on the spiritual side of fasting and all that it was doing in my soul that it took me a while to realize the physical benefits. On top of that, it broke my coffee habit. It was through fasting that I learned more about myself. I recovered my childhood innocence, love and trust. I found myself in Adoration crying out of love for Jesus, just like I had when I was a young girl. Fasting has opened the door to a new freedom of being who I really am: Darcie, a daughter of God.

All fasting leads to the Eucharist. Wednesday and Friday sandwich Thursday, which is traditionally the day of the Eucharist. This practice goes back to the early Church teaching in the Didache when Christians fasted on Wednesday to prepare for receiving the body, blood, soul and divinity of Jesus in Communion, and in commemoration of the betrayal of Judas. And then on Friday they fasted in thanksgiving for having received the Eucharist, and in commemoration of the Crucifixion of Jesus. In Gaelic, Wednesday actually means "little fast" and Friday means "big fast." Fasting detaches us from this world and prayer reattaches us to heaven. Fasting is our means to live in the truth that we are pilgrims on a journey and that our homeland is heaven.

Only once we're in heaven will we understand how our seemingly small sacrifices opened the door for abundant graces. It's ok if you haven't been a good faster. Our Lady invites us to try fasting again. Even if it's in a very small way. Our Lady reminds us that "Only by prayer and fasting can war be stopped" (April 25, 1992).

In Scripture, Jesus, Moses and Elijah are the only three prophets who fasted for 40 days. Has anyone ever noticed that they are also the three seen conversing during the Transfiguration of Jesus? There are special graces for those who fast. We have this opportunity every Lent, as well as during Advent and Ordinary Time throughout the Church year. When we deny ourselves, we put God in the first place in our lives. We need this practice as we journey on our conversion because there will continue to be many temptations. The late Father Slavko Barbaric was a Franciscan priest and spiritual director of the visionaries in Medjugorje. He also wrote about fasting and guided fasting retreats. He said:

> "The deepest longing of man's heart is actually for peace. In everything we do, whether good or bad, we seek peace. When a person loves, looks for, and experiences peace — or even when he hates and wants revenge — he seeks peace. When he stays sober or fights against addiction, he seeks peace. When he becomes drunk, he also seeks peace. When he fights for his life and the lives of those he loves, he realizes peace . . . Therefore, every decision of man is, in

its essence, a decision for peace . . . It is therefore, through fasting that a person comes to understand what he must fight against in himself. In this way, our subconscious is also freed from everything that drives us to restlessness and disorder. The soul then becomes still and conditions for peace are realized."[4]

So as you clean out and clear out your stuff, and clean out and clear out your body through fasting, you are creating the conditions for freedom, detachment, and peace.

Now that you're ready to start fasting, here are some practical ways to actually begin.

Whether you're an experienced faster, a new faster or a fallen-off-the-wagon-but-trying-again faster (like most of us are), there is a starting point for you. (Check out there flowchart on page 62.) We come from different walks of life and of faith, which is why some people will be able to jump right into the bread and water fast twice a week and others that may need to start by just eliminating snacks two days a week. The range of "starts" is as numerous as there are individuals. The important point is that you start. Through prayer and discernment with the Lord, He will guide you on how to start.

The Lord knows you, your strengths, your weaknesses, your personality and he knows the future with as much confidence as he knows the present and the past. Pray to the Holy Spirit for the gift of knowledge. Ask The Lord for his help that you may better understand yourself and how he is calling you to begin fasting.

Know that The Lord's invitation is not only to fast, but to pray. He is calling you to a more profound relationship with him.

The key is to start incrementally. Just as one wouldn't go to the gym for

---

[4] Fr. Slavko Barbaric, Fast with the Heart, trans. Rita Falsetto (Medjugorje: Informativni Centar Mir, 2003), 103-104.

the first time and try bench-pressing 300 pounds, the same is true for fasting. Fasting muscles need to be trained, strengthened and stretched. Fasting is a journey and takes time, perseverance and most importantly, patience.

Due to our sinful human nature, there will be times when we fail or feel like we failed. Do not fall into the trap of discouragement! "Fasting just isn't for me. I'm not a faster." These are deceitful thoughts and do not come from The Lord. Bring this to Jesus and He will transform them into hope. Remember that all fasting is pleasing to The Lord.

If you find yourself going through the motions, discouraged or without peace, it is most likely because there's insufficient time spent in prayer. Fasting and prayer go hand in hand and if you pray well, you will fast well and if you fast well, you will pray well. I can tell you right now the reason for all my fasts that ended early, were weak or felt incomplete was due to not praying enough. Fasting detaches us from earth and prayer attaches us to heaven. We need to fill the void fasting leaves with prayer.

How to prepare for a fast day

Preparation for a fast day begins the evening before. Spend some time in prayer and with The Lord, determine if you will complete a 12-hour, 18-hour or 24-hour fast. Ask the Lord to prepare your heart, your mind and your body.

On the morning of the fast day begin by praying. Take your time when you add your intentions. The more specific they are, the more you'll be grounded in them and find the strength to fast for them later in the day. Perhaps even write them down. Call on the Holy Spirit to fill your heart and mind with intentions. What's heavy on your heart? What needs healing? Who would you pray for if you knew it was your last time praying for them?

How you start your fast day will greatly impact the rest of your day. Be sure to relay any thoughts, worries, concerns, excitements you might have about fasting that day to the Good Lord. Call on the Holy Spirit for enlightenment to what graces you need. Thank God for calling you closer to Him through fasting. Thank God for the gift of being His child.

Once you've prayed, then enjoy your bread. Be sure to take small bites and chew each time for 45-60 seconds. Digestion begins in the mouth!

If you can, attend Holy Mass. The Bread of Life is the source of great strength. Eucharistic Adoration is another opportunity. As you pray throughout the day, recall and repeat your prayer intentions, especially when you are tempted or distracted.

There will be a moment during the day when you think it's your breaking point, and you think you can't go on... this is Calvary. Persevere! This is the time to go to your knees and pray. Completely surrender to God and His Holy Will. Invoke the intercession of the Blessed Mother, your guardian angel and all the saints. In these moments you can also read the Holy Bible for strength and inspiration. You will then experience grace and you will receive peace. Continue to pray and to recall your prayer intentions and those of the community. Smile!

As the fasting day comes to a close, thank the Lord for the gift of fasting, His strength and everything you experienced this day. Journal your thoughts, feelings and desires. Pray that He may seal all the graces given to you.

If you are breaking the fast at 12pm or 6pm, we recommend praying in thanksgiving first. Then, prepare a meal that's easy to digest. A smoothie, grilled fish or chicken would be a healthy option.

Sometimes I find it best to break the fast with a small piece of fruit and then wait a while to have a meal. This way, the fast has been completed peacefully and then you can prayerfully decide what to eat based on physical need, not emotional want. Our bodies are a temple for the Holy Spirit.

Remember that you don't need to compensate for what you didn't have while fasting. (Or eat more in preparation for fasting.) Remain in a spirit of thanksgiving and this will help your self control. Having a fasting friend and breaking the fast in a community will help.

Temptations on fast days

As you fast, you will find that temptations may seem stronger than ever and that's because they are. It was only when Jesus went into the desert and fasted for 40 days that he was first tempted three times by Satan, so we can most certainly expect the same, even the exact same temptations.

Just like Jesus, Satan will tempt your hunger. "If you are the Son of God, command that these stones become loaves of bread" (Matthew 4:3). Perhaps it will sound more like, "if you're really going to fast today, you will still need coffee." Or maybe "Just a little peanut butter on your bread won't make a difference. You must be so hungry!" Thankfully, Jesus overcame this temptation and we too can over come it and pray His words, "It is written: 'One does not live by bread alone, but by every word that comes forth from the mouth of God.'" In moments of hunger and temptation, let us turn to the Holy Bible and dine on His Word. Even more so, we can attend Holy Mass and Adoration to encounter and receive the Risen Lord, and to turn to Him for strength.

In Jesus' second temptation Satan says, "If you are the Son of God, throw yourself down. For it is written: 'He will command his angels concerning you and with their hands they will support you, lest you dash your foot against a stone'" (Matthew 4:6). This is a temptation to test God or to test our trust in God. Maybe it'd sound like, "You're fasting aren't you? Getting closer to God, yet you just found out that terrible news. Are you sure God loves you?" Or maybe, "I'm late to work so I'll speed on the highway, God won't let anything bad happen to me." Sound all too familiar? Let us thank Jesus for His example, for His response, "Again it is written, 'You shall not put the Lord, your God, to the test.'" We too can pray and overcome this temptation and say to God, "Lord, I will not put you to the test and I trust in Your Will and plan for me."

In the third temptation, Jesus is confronted with false worship. "All these [kingdoms of the world] I shall give to you, if you will prostrate yourself and worship me." Maybe it'd sound like, "Fasting isn't going to help you or your intentions. You need more money and a bigger house to really solve your problems." Or even, "You can fast next week, or another day. It doesn't need to happen right now." In moments that start to pull us away from focusing on God and His Will, let us place ourselves at the foot of the cross and look up at our crucified Jesus who loves us so much. We can also pray Jesus' words in such temptations, "Get away, Satan! It is written: 'The Lord, your God, shall you worship and him alone shall you serve.'" By choosing God, we love Him and serve Him. Let God rule in our hearts, minds, bodies and spirits.

After the third temptation, it says, "Then the devil left him and, behold, angels came and ministered to him" (Matthew 4:10-11). Angels came and ministered to Him, would the same not be true for us? If we're fasting and experiencing the same temptations as Jesus Christ, we know too that angels will come and minister to us. What a grace and blessing! In all of these temptations, there is a common theme: Satan trying to ruin our relationship with God, trying to rob us of our identity as Children of God, as disciples of Jesus Christ.

Let us remember that Jesus is our guide and our friend, and that He overcame all of these temptations and He wants to help us overcome ours. He is with us and in us when we fast. Let us not be afraid to call on Him during times of temptation and to pray His prayers, especially the Our Father. Jesus is victorious over Satan through His prayers and fasting, and the same is true for us.

"Jesus said to them, 'My food is to do the will of the one who sent me and to finish his work'" (John 4:34).

Questions for Your Personal Reflection

1. What am I holding onto because of the status it gives me? What does this tell me about what I treasure?

2. How will I begin clearing out my living space? Where do I want to start? Can I find ways of using this process to be more charitable to the poor?

3. How can I try to start fasting? Can I start with fasting one day a week or one day a month? What concerns are holding me back?

Questions for Small Group Discussion

1. What's going to be my approach to clearing out my belongings?
2. How will I maintain simplicity and order afterwards?
3. What is my attitude towards fasting?
4. What are some ways I can be sure to follow through on my fast?

Action Item

Choose a fasting accountability partner for fast days. Organize a group yard sale or donation day.

How should I start fasting?

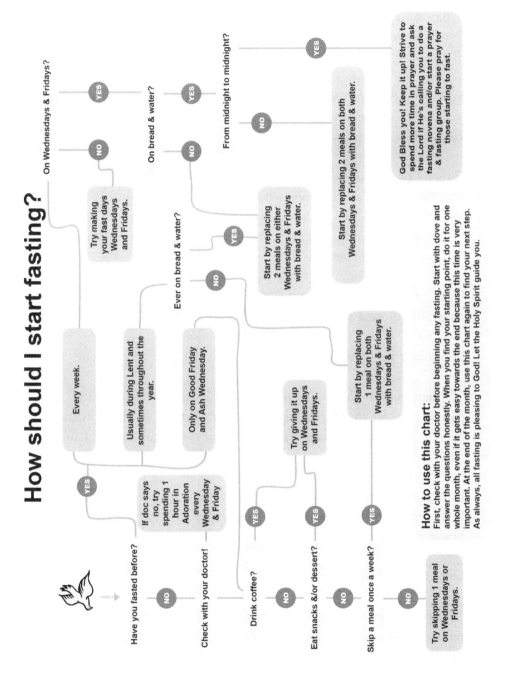

How to use this chart:
First, check with your doctor before beginning any fasting. Start with dove and answer the questions honestly. When you find your starting point, do it for one whole month, even if it gets easy towards the end because this time is very important. At the end of the month, use this chart again to find your next step. As always, all fasting is pleasing to God! Let the Holy Spirit guide you.

Fasting Prayer on a Fast Day

Father, today I resolve to fast. I choose to fast because your prophets fasted, because your Son, Jesus Christ, fasted, as did His apostles and disciples.

I decide to fast because your servant, Mother Mary also fasted. I fast today as a disciple of your Son and I ask for the intercession of the saints and my guardian angel.

Father, I present this day of fasting to you for the ability to discover your Word more and discover what is essential and non-essential in this life. I present this fast to you for Peace—for peace in my heart, peace with my family, peace with my neighbors, peace in my town/city, state and my country.

I fast for peace in the world, for all troubled spots in the world. I remember those who are hungry and impoverished.

I fast today for (your intentions).

Through this fast cleanse me of all bad habits and calm down my passions and let your virtues increase in me. Let the depth of my soul open to your grace through this fast, so that it may totally affect and cleanse me.

Father, please help me fast with my heart. Mary, you were free in your heart and bound to nothing except the Father's will. Please obtain by prayer the grace of a joyful fast for me today.

Our Father…Hail Mary…Glory Be! Amen.

* Adapted from "Fast with the Heart" fasting prayer by Father Slavko Barbaric. Used with permission from *Live the Fast*.

Heaven on Earth

Chapter 6

I have found heaven on earth. His name is Jesus Christ in the Eucharist. The Eucharist has always captivated me. I remember preparing for my First Holy Communion and understanding that it was truly Jesus, not a representation, but actually Jesus. I remember being taught to have an open heart to receive him and that he is love itself. At eight years old, I would kneel in church looking at the elevated host and know it was him. I think this is why I have always tried to go to Mass, no matter how far I was from God. This must have been a gift from Our Lady because she said in part of her January 25, 1998 message, "May Holy Mass, little children, not be a habit for you, but life. By living Holy Mass each day, you will feel the need for holiness, and you will grow in holiness."

There will come a point in our journey when we need to seriously ask ourselves, "Is Jesus truly present in the Blessed Sacrament?" Our answer will define how we live. There is no gray area here. There aren't any maybes, sometimes or it depends. There can be only one of two answers: yes or no. We each need to answer this question for ourselves and own it. In the Catholic faith, we believe, yes, Jesus is truly present in the Blessed Sacrament: body, blood, soul and divinity. The Lord said, "Amen, amen, I say to you, unless you eat the flesh of the Son of Man and drink his blood, you do not have life within you. Whoever eats my flesh and drinks my blood has eternal life, and I will raise him on the last day" (John 6:53-54). In Holy Mass, we do just that. We consume the body and blood of Jesus Christ. In him, we are given eternal life. This is the most beautiful part of our faith! Other Christian denominations have bread and wine as a representation of Jesus, but it's not Jesus and the Lord's words are very clear to "eat the flesh of the Son of Man and drink his blood." Later in this Scripture passage, we are told that some disciples left because they found this to be a "hard saying." We can ask ourselves, do we find this to be a hard saying too, or do we accept it?

Other food we consume is processed by our bodies and becomes part of us, but not the Eucharist. In a vision St. Augustine had, Jesus said to him, "You will not change me into yourself like bodily food; but you will be changed into me."[5] When we receive Holy Communion, Jesus transforms our lowly selves into his glorious self.

If we truly believed this, would we not attend daily Mass, go to Adoration and even make visits to him in the tabernacle? Would we not have the utmost reverence and respect in church, where he dwells in the tabernacle? Would we not want to have a clean and pure heart to receive the King of Kings? Would we not change out of our sweatpants, jeans and sweatshirts before going to Mass? Would we not be at Mass early and on time to prepare for this divine encounter? Would we not do everything we could to get our family members and friends there?

Perhaps we need a little more umph. We'll go to a story. In 750 AD, a monastic priest was celebrating Holy Mass in Lanciano, Italy, and doubted the real presence of Jesus in the Eucharist. During the Consecration, the bread and wine literally turned into flesh and blood. All those attending the Mass saw the flesh and blood, and the relics of this Eucharist are still intact today. Of course, testing has been done on them and the findings were as follows:

- The flesh is real flesh. The blood is real blood.
- The flesh and the blood belong to the human species.
- The flesh consists of the muscular tissue of the heart.
- The flesh section consists of: the myocardium, the

---

[5] Saint Augustine, Confessions, trans. Carolyn J.-B. Hammond (Cambridge: Harvard University Press, 2014), VII, 18.

endocardium, the vagus nerve and also the left ventricle of the heart for the large thickness of the myocardium.
- The flesh is a "HEART" complete in its essential structure.
- The flesh and the blood have the same blood type: AB (Blood-type identical to that which Prof. Baima Bollone uncovered in the Holy Shroud of Turin).
- The blood contained proteins in the same normal proportions (percentage-wise) that are found in the sero-proteic make-up of fresh normal blood.
- The blood also contained these minerals: chlorides, phosphorus, magnesium, potassium, sodium and calcium.
- The preservation of the flesh and of the flood, which were left in their natural state for twelve centuries and exposed to the action of atmospheric and biological agents, remains an extraordinary phenomenon.[6]

This is one of 153 approved Eucharistic miracles worldwide. Sometimes, God slightly lifts the veil to remind us of the truth of his son in the Eucharist.

It is no wonder then that the evil one would hate the Eucharist. It is also no wonder that satanists conduct black masses with stolen hosts. In a conversation with a former satanist, a priest asked him about the Holy Eucharist. Specifically, the priest asked him if someone were to put ten identical communion hosts in front of him (before his conversion) — with nine being unconsecrated and one consecrated — would he be able to identify the consecrated host? The former satanist immediately said he could. "The priest asked him in amazement, 'But how were you able to know?!?' He looked at me and the words he spoke are forever burned in my memory: 'Because of the hate,' he said. 'Because of the burning hate I would feel toward that host, apart from all the others.' "[7]

---

[6] "Eucharistic Miracle: Lanciano, Italy 8th Century A.D.," Therealpresence.org, accessed 25 April, 2016. <http://www.therealpresence.org/eucharst/mir/lanciano.html/> Used with permission.

[7] Fr. Andrew Trapp, "Satanism and the Eucharist" in Saint Factory: God wants to make you a saint (blog), accessed 24 April, 2004. <http://saintfactory.com/satanism-the-eucharist/>

This scenario poses a burning question in our hearts. If someone were to put ten identical communion hosts in front of us, nine unconsecrated and one consecrated, would we be able to identify the consecrated host? Would we recognize Jesus? Do we desire to love Him more in this sacrament?

Our devotion to Jesus in the Eucharist will set our lukewarm hearts on fire with love. We must avoid being lukewarm because, as Scripture cautions, "So, because you are lukewarm, neither hot nor cold, I will spit you out of my mouth" (Revelation 3:16). If we're in love with Jesus, then we're in love with the Holy Mass. The more we fall in love with the Holy Mass, the more we fall in love with Jesus. Our Lady tells us, "What I want from you is to show me your love by coming to Mass, and the Lord will reward you abundantly" (November 21, 1985). Love and Holy Mass go hand in hand. St. John of Vianney said, "If we really understood the Mass, we would die of joy." Holy Mass is heaven on Earth. St. Faustina beautifully wrote that she doesn't envy the angels because Jesus's blood mingles with ours.[8]

The best way to begin is by going to Mass an additional day besides Sunday. Maybe you can start with one or two day days during the week and gradually add the others, like I did. It is possible to make it part of your daily life (with kids, work and all). Maybe you don't think you have time, but we always have time for the things we love. It's not a question of time, it's a question of love. Even if you don't love Mass yet, let the desire to love it bring you there. Our Lady tells us, "Dear children! I wish to call you to a living of the Holy Mass. There are many of you who have sensed the beauty of the Holy Mass, but there are also those who come unwillingly. I have chosen you, dear children, but Jesus gives you his graces in the Mass. Therefore, consciously live the Holy Mass and let your coming to it be a joyful one. Come to it with love and make the Mass your own. Thank you for having responded to my call" (April 3,1986).

---

[8] Saint Faustina, Diary of Saint Maria Faustina Kowalska: Divine Mercy in My Soul, (Stockbridge, MA: Marian Press, 2005), 133.

A huge turning point in my personal understanding of Mass was when I learned that it is both timeless and changeless. During the Consecration, we are present at the Last Supper, the Crucifixion and the Resurrection of Jesus. We are at the table with the disciples as Jesus says to us, "Take and eat; this is my body" (Jesus, Matthew 26:26). We are at the foot of Calvary with Mother Mary and St. John as Jesus commends his spirit into his father's hands and breathes his last. We are there at the tomb when his body is resurrected. Mind blowing. I know this knowledge changed how I attended and participated in Mass. It became alive. And not only that, but my participation mattered. My prayers are united with Jesus on the cross during Mass. When I also learned that our guardian angels bring up our petitions to the altar, I was sure to be early to Mass, even just a few minutes, to identify my petitions. All heaven is present during Mass: the angels, saints, Our Lady and Our Lord. Have you ever just imagined what that looks like during Mass? Holy Mass is why Jesus could say, "I am with you always, until the end of world "(Matthew 28:20).

My love for Adoration was sparked in Medjugorje on my first trip in 2010. They had a beautiful evening prayer program. The monstrance was decorated with Mary holding Jesus, and the consecrated Host was right at the center where their hearts would be. Heavenly music would play, followed by reflections from a priest and then periods of silence. The priest would kneel in front of the Blessed Sacrament for two or three hours. I was amazed by his posture, reverence and attentiveness. Watching the priest, along with thousands of pilgrims kneeling on crushed stone as they adored Jesus in the Blessed Sacrament, made me want to love him more. The reflections from the priest weren't really reflections at all, but conversations with Jesus. The priest led us into sacred ground where we felt free and at peace to converse with Our Lord. It was there and then that I learned to speak to Jesus from my heart and to listen to him. Mind you, I had to get over my thoughts wandering and my aching knees' desire to constantly change positions. The priest began:

"Jesus I adore you. I believe that you are true God and true man hidden in this Consecrated Host because you said, 'This is My Body given up for you.' I want to adore you, the Heavenly Bread. I ask you to remove from me everything that still hinders me from meeting you in this Host; from meeting you, the Living and True God, Emmanuel - God, who decided to remain with us in this simple way. At this moment, I have decided to be with you. Quiet my thoughts and feelings and direct my desires to you. Grant that I may be completely still before you."[9]

In Adoration, we learn to be our true selves because we cannot hide anything from the Lord, and, more importantly, we learn how much he loves us. Even in our weaknesses and failures, Jesus loves us. That is why he said, "Those who are well do not need a physician, but the sick do. I did not come to call the righteous but sinners" (Mark 2:17). Adoration became part of my life. While I was living in Boston, I would walk to a perpetual Adoration shrine. I would spend hours in front of Our Lord. As a friend once said, time in Adoration is like time in the sun in that you don't realize you got burned until in the evening. You don't realize the graces and transformation in your soul until later (sometimes way later) after time spent in Adoration. Our Lady encourages us to go to Adoration, "Dear children! I call you to work on your personal conversion. You are still far from meeting with God in your heart. Therefore, spend all the more time in prayer and Adoration of Jesus in the Most Blessed Sacrament of the Altar, for him to change you and to put into your hearts a living faith and a desire for eternal life. Everything is passing, little children; only God is not passing. I am with you, and I encourage you with love. Thank you for having responded to my call" (March 25, 2008).

I'm thankful for writing this book because it pushed me to spend more time in Adoration (even with two little kids). How could I write more about Our Lord if I didn't spend more time in his presence? The night

---

[9] Fr. Slavko Barbaric, Fast with the Heart, trans. Rita Falsetto (Medjugorje: Informativni Centar Mir, 2003), 174.

Jesus was handed over, he asked his disciples to keep watch with him. But three times he went back and found them sleeping. He said to his disciples, "The spirit is willing, but the flesh is weak" (Matthew 26:41). We can often find excuses not to go to Adoration, and they're usually ones of the flesh: too tired, too hungry, or too busy. But Jesus had asked the disciples, "So you could not keep watch with me for one hour?" (Matthew 26:40). Jesus asks us this question now. Could we not spend one hour (a week) with him? Our Lady told us in her March 15, 1984 message, "Tonight also, dear children, I am grateful to you in a special way for being here. Unceasingly adore the Most Blessed Sacrament of the Altar. I am always present when the faithful are adoring. Special graces are then being received."

I'll never forget the funny story of my dad asking my mom where I was one evening (this was shortly before I began discerning religious life), and my mom said "Adoration." He was exasperated, "Adoration! Adoration! Adoration! That's all she does!" I only came across this quote later, but it would have been perfect for this scenario, "The time you spend with Jesus in the Blessed Sacrament is the best time you will spend on Earth. Each moment that you spend with Jesus will deepen your union with him and make your soul everlastingly more glorious and beautiful in heaven, and will help bring about everlasting peace on Earth" (St. Mother Teresa of Calcutta).

We find ourselves wanting to acknowledge Jesus in the tabernacles more often too. Whether it's an actual visit or simple blessing oneself when driving by a church. These little gestures must delight Our Lord so much. St. Josemaria said, "When you approach the tabernacle, remember that he has been waiting for you for twenty centuries."

Our Lady once told the visionaries that if they have the choice to see her in an apparition or go to Holy Mass, they should go to Holy Mass. The Most Holy Eucharist is the center of our Catholic faith, but is it the center of our lives?

"For my flesh is true food, and my blood is true drink. Whoever eats my flesh and drinks my blood remains in me and I in him" (John 6:55-56).

Questions for Your Personal Reflection

1. What is keeping me from attending Mass more frequently? Can I make modifications to my schedule to place more importance on the Mass, either by attending more frequently or by arriving earlier?
2. Do I really believe Jesus is present in the Eucharist? How will I change how I approach Mass? What can I do to better prepare to meet Him in the Eucharist each week?
3. What is keeping me from wanting to know Jesus more? Am I afraid of what He will ask of me?

Questions for Small Group Discussion

1. How has my prayer changed since becoming more aware of Jesus in the Eucharist?
2. What am I learning about Jesus and myself?
3. When did I first become aware that the Eucharist was really Jesus?

Action Item

Read "In Sinu Jesu: When Heart Speaks to Heart – The Journal of a Priest at Prayer," and then spend an hour in Adoration.

Speaking with God

Chapter 7

By no means do I feel qualified to write a chapter on prayer, but I trust the Holy Spirit to inspire my writing and help me know what needs to be included.

With that said, I'd like to begin this chapter with a prayer to the Holy Spirit:

Come Holy Spirit, fill the hearts of your faithful and kindle in them the fire of your love. Send forth your Spirit and they shall be created. And you shall renew the face of the earth. O, God, who by the light of the Holy Spirit, did instruct the hearts of the faithful, grant that by the same Holy Spirit we may be truly wise and ever enjoy his consolations, through Christ Our Lord. Amen.

We have a tendency to overthink and, therefore, complicate many things in life, and prayer is certainly one of them. We can question if we're praying "right" or praying enough. Every once in awhile, we see someone in church and think, "Ah, they know how to pray." We can ask ourselves, "Do I even know how to pray?" and "What is prayer?" Let's not complicate things. Prayer is simple. St. Jane Frances de Chantal said beautifully, "Follow your own way of speaking to Our Lord sincerely, lovingly, confidently and simply, as your heart dictates."

Learning to pray from the heart is an ongoing process. We learn to pray better by praying more. Our Lady can't seem to say it enough in her messages, "Pray, pray, pray." What I find most amazing is that she also tells us, "Prayer works miracles in you and through you" (October 25, 2013). Our Lady knows our hearts, and even answers our question about why we need to pray. In her September 13, 1984 message she explained, "Dear children! I still need your prayers. You wonder why all these prayers? Look around you, dear children, and you will see how greatly sin has dominated the world. Pray, therefore, that Jesus conquers. Thank you for having responded to my call."

We can learn from Jesus, who went off to pray alone many times in his years of ministry. He is our example in all things. We also need to go off alone to pray. We need to find that quiet space and time each day. I once heard that our souls can be compared to reflecting pools. Our lives are to reflect Jesus. If our souls, like reflecting pools, are constantly getting ripples from the vibration of voices and are splashed about with anxieties, then our reflection of Jesus becomes distorted and, in some cases, not even recognizable. We need that personal quiet time with the Lord, and it may be difficult because we're not used to it. Our Lady also reminds us to have silent time with God: "Dear children! Today I am calling you to renew your hearts. Open yourselves to God and surrender to him all your difficulties and crosses so God may turn everything into joy. Little children, you cannot open yourselves to God if you do not pray. Therefore, from today decide to consecrate a time in the day only for an encounter with God in silence. In that way you will be able, with God, to witness my presence here. Little children, I do not wish to force you. Rather freely give God your time, like children of God. Thank you for having responded to my call" (July 25, 1989).

Our culture is filled with noise, and even in our relationships with loved ones, there are many distractions. How often are phones at the dinner table or background music on or text messages being checked during a conversation? If it's become so difficult to communicate with the ones we love, physically in front of us, then how much harder is it to communicate with God in our hearts? There's a story in Scripture about the Lord asking the prophet Elijah to go stand on the mountain before the Lord and he would pass by. Then came a strong and violent wind, crushing rocks, an earthquake, and a fire, but the Lord wasn't in any of these. How did the Lord speak to Elijah? ". . . after the fire, a light silent sound. When he heard this, Elijah hid his face in his cloak and went out and stood at the entrance of the cave. A voice said to him, Why are you here, Elijah?" (1 Kings 19:11-13). Very often we want God to speak loudly in our lives. We want that earthquake or fire, and when we don't get it, we think he's not speaking to us. But we need to be reminded through this Scripture passage that God's voice is "a light silent sound."

We need silence to hear his voice. Specifically, we need silence in our hearts. The noise around us disrupts us, but not nearly as much as we do ourselves. Letting our imaginations, thoughts and emotions run in all directions can keep our hearts busy and full of noise. Learning to have silence in our hearts to hear God takes practice, but once we have it, we have also learned how to keep it.

If we were away from the church for a while, there can be a tendency to stay on the surface level of our prayer. We stick to our list of intentions, we thank God and we tell him we love him. We know we are loved by him. We think everything is just dandy, yet our hearts are yearning for more. We're afraid to let God into the places of pain. We're afraid to visit them again with him because we think we'll hurt again. We have a mindset that since we were away from God that he was away from us. This is not the truth. No matter how far we strayed from God, he never left us. He has been with us always, and in prayer he wants to show you in a special way that he was there when you needed him the most. He was there when you were suffering the most. He was there when you thought no one else was. He was there. He always has been and always will be. Also, Our Lady has always been with us. She tells us, "I, the Mother, love you all. And in any moment that is difficult for you, do not be afraid because I love you even then when you are far from me and my Son" (May 24, 1984).

In prayer, we encounter God and God is truth. And sometimes we don't like hearing the truth. It happened to me just recently. While in mental prayer, I shared with God some frustrations I'd been having and that I felt let down by him (seemingly) in a particular circumstance. He answered me, "You are frustrated and upset because your expectations weren't met." At that I was done praying for the moment. I didn't want to face the truth. I didn't want to accept that my disappointment was caused by my unreasonable expectations, even though I realized it was true. So yes, we can harden our hearts when we hear his voice.

Maybe that's why we don't like to pray sometimes. Because we know we'll encounter the truth and the truth changes us. The truth invites us to live differently than we had been previously. The truth causes us to see ourselves as we really are: sinners — weak, broken human beings. We forget that God already knows that. He knows everything about us. And more importantly, he loves us even in our weakness and littleness. It can be humbling to encounter the truth. And sometimes we don't want to be humble!

So just when we think God's not speaking to us, maybe it's because we're not listening. God is always speaking to us. Scripture tells us, "And your ears shall hear a word behind you: 'This is the way; walk in it,' when you would turn to the right or the left" (Isaiah 30:21). God speaks to us more often than we realize. Our Lady encourages us too: "Dear children! I call you to work on your personal conversion. You are still far from meeting with God in your heart. Therefore, spend all the more time in prayer and adoration of Jesus in the Most Blessed Sacrament of the altar, for him to change you and to put into your hearts a living faith and a desire for eternal life. Everything is passing, little children; only God is not passing. I am with you, and I encourage you with love. Thank you for having responded to my call" (March 25, 2008).

Opening up the depths of our hearts to God in prayer is sometimes like pulling off a Band-Aid. We all have Band-Aids on our souls that we've kept on too long; wounds that we thought we could "take care of ourselves." We put the Band-Aid on and just let them heal. We'd sometimes go to take the Band-Aid off, but think "it needs more time to heal." Meanwhile, the wound underneath hasn't gotten air so it's become infected. The pain of the infection is what reminds us that the wound is still there. It still hurts. So when we let God take the Band-Aid off, he is able to wash it clean and heal it through his Holy Spirit. What is the main requirement for washing something clean? Water. And guess how that "water" is released? Tears. So do not be surprised if you cry or even ball out loud when God washes your wounds. There is healing taking place. The more we let God into all the areas of our hearts, then the more he is able to dwell in us more fully. This desire and willingness to surrender to God is what we strive for in prayer. We have great moments of surrender in our lives, but we also have moments that we hang onto ourselves. We need prayer to learn how to let go. Just to note — the gift of tears is from the Holy Spirit. A Catholic News Agency article recounted Pope Francis' words about the gift of tears:

> All of us have felt joy, sadness and sorrow in our lives,' but 'have we wept during the darkest moment? Have we had that gift of tears that prepares the eyes to look, to see the Lord?' the Pope asked. 'We too can ask the Lord for the gift of tears,' he said. 'It is a beautiful grace … to weep praying for everything: for what is good, for our sins, for graces, for joy itself.' Weeping, the Holy Father explained, 'prepares us to see Jesus.[10]

In a mysterious way, when we revisit places of suffering with God and he brings us healing, there is often a revelation of what our personal mission is. The healing and consolation we received in our suffering is being passed onto our brothers and sisters who are experiencing the

---

[10] CNA/EWTN News, "Pope Francis asks for 'gift of tears' to see Risen Christ." Catholic News Agency. Last modified 3 April, 2013.
< http://www.catholicnewsagency.com/news/pope-francis-asks-for-gift-of-tears-to-see-risen-christ/>

same suffering. As St. Paul beautifully said, "Blessed be the God and Father of our Lord Jesus Christ, the Father of compassion and God of all encouragement, who encourages us in our every affliction, so that we may be able to encourage those who are in any affliction with the encouragement with which we ourselves are encouraged by God" (2 Corinthians 1:3-4). Imagine that, the healing and encouragement from our past pains and sufferings are what God wants you to use to bring others to Jesus and to glorify him.

I couldn't give a better example of this mission than the writing of this book. Like I said in my *Dear Friend* chapter, when I was going through the healing and purification of my past pains, sufferings and sins, I had no intention of sharing it with others. I received my encouragement and I wanted to keep it for myself. It was in prayer that the Lord asked me to share what I had received. He gave me opportunities to speak at retreats when I worked at *Live the Fast*. A little bit at a time, I surrendered. I would also write a bi-weekly email to the *Live the Fast* community members encouraging them in their prayer and fasting. Every time I hit "send," I wasn't sure if what I wrote would be of any help. But then the responses would come in. "How did you know?! This is exactly what I'm experiencing." And others, "Thank you for these words of encouragement." God used this feedback to reassure me that this was his will for me.

It was in Adoration after returning from Medjugorje that the Lord inspired me to write a book. I remember thinking that I was too young to be writing a book about one's faith journey considering I still have a ways to go. Yet the Lord reminded me of all that I experienced. The seed to write a book was planted in my heart. I was to answer the question, "So you went to Medjugorje and you're back, now what?" It became clear that the encouragement and blessings I received from the Lord were to be shared with others. We also see this happen in the tomb where Jesus was laid. We often think of it as a place of mourning, but we forget that it was in that tomb that Jesus resurrected.

So what does God want to resurrect in your life? What is his will for you? What does he want you to share? Why did he create you the way you are? How does God want to bring your experiences, sufferings and joys together for his purpose? You've probably started asking these questions along your journey and that's beautiful. It's crossing the threshold from just desiring to receive to desiring to give. Prayer is where we can bring these questions to God and ask him. He will answer us. Not only does he speak to us in the depths of our hearts, but also in his Word, the Scriptures.

I had always heard it was important to read the Bible and to know the Bible, but it really wasn't until I went to Medjugorje that I learned just how life giving it is. Reading Scripture daily is one of the five stones Our Lady identifies. In her August 25, 1993 message she said, "Dear children! I want you to understand that I am your Mother, that I want to help you and call you to prayer. Only by prayer can you understand and accept my messages and practice them in your life. Read Sacred Scripture, live it, and pray to understand the signs of the times. This is a special time; therefore, I am with you to draw you close to my heart and the heart of my Son Jesus. Dear little children, I want you to be children of the light and not of darkness. Therefore, live what I am telling you. Thank you for having responded to my call."

Our Lady at Medjugorje even asked families to keep the Bible in a visible place of honor in the home, so we are more inclined to read it. We need the Word of God in our hearts and our minds because it's the truth, which combats the lies we're constantly being told by the evil one. Jesus is the "Word made flesh." No matter where we are on our faith journey, we all need time with the Word of God *daily*. I must admit that this was probably the hardest stone for me to truly live. I approached reading Scripture like it was any other book. Of course there would be things that struck me, encouraged me or comforted me, but I would get kind of stuck. Not only that, I thought it depended on me. In some way, I thought I had to dissect the Scripture and extract the message God was trying to give me. Sounds like a lot of work, right? No wonder it was exhausting and something that I avoided instead of looked forward to! However, I remember I would keep coming back to one of Our Lady messages, "Pray, little children, that prayer may become life for you. In this way, in your life you will discover the peace and joy which God gives to those who have an open heart to his love" (August 25, 2007). I wanted prayer to become life for me, not a burden.

Thankfully I started to learn how to *pray* with Scripture when I was with Mother Olga. I was introduced to *Lectio Divina,* also known as Divine Reading. The best two books I can recommend on learning to pray with Scripture are by Fr. Timothy M. Gallagher, O.M.V. titled, "Meditation and Contemplation: An Ignatian Guide to Praying with Scripture" and "An Ignatian Introduction to Prayer: Scriptural Reflections According to the *Spiritual Exercises.*" This way of praying with the Scripture has transformed my prayer. I learned that I could use my imagination to enter the Bible passages and see and hear Jesus. We spend time together and have conversations. What I also love is that I can go back to this encounter with Jesus throughout the rest of the day and am filled with His presence and love. Praying with Scripture really did become a joy for me and something I look forward to. I try to write down a sentence or two reflecting about our time together.

This is where journaling comes in. A journal can start simply by writing down Scripture passages that speak to us. Maybe it's from Holy Mass or a Bible study or something online. When we start collecting these Scripture passages, we can then take a couple minutes to reflect on them and journal our thoughts. Why did this passage strike me? Does it bother me? What did it remind me of? What do I hear God saying to me in it? How can I apply it to my life? Before long, we will have a collection of, essentially, conversations between God and ourselves. This is so important because we have a tendency to forget. We might have the best memory in the world, but when we are in a period of desolation (aridity, feeling far from God), we cannot seem to remember what consolation was like. We cannot seem to remember what it's like to be close to God and it's difficult. If we have a journal, we have physical proof. We can go back and read and see our conversation with God. We are reminded, and sometimes that is all we need to get through the desolation. So if you haven't journaled — start. If you stopped journaling, start again. It doesn't take much time — five or 10 minutes a few days a week. If you're feeling stuck, there are even journal entry prompts that you can find online.

Like I shared in the beginning of the book, it was because of my journaling in high school that I started seeking a relationship with God again. It was very simple. I wrote to him as my friend. I shared my worries, concerns, hopes and desires. Getting specific and honest helped me see how God was working in my life. I started to notice that what I thought were "coincidences" were in fact Divine Providence. Through journaling, I was opening myself up to God and that's what he needs from us — an open heart.

Another wonderful aspect of journaling is record keeping. We can look back and see the prayers God answered. Again, we are so quick to forget that we passed that exam or got that raise or that a relative was healed. We can also write down our sins for confession and then be able to review them and see what we've overcome by God's grace, and also what we still need help with a few months later. Our journal can have many purposes and can evolve as our prayer life does. There's no "right" way to journal. It is between you and God. Journaling is a prayer. Many saints throughout Church history kept spiritual journals that are now published. I highly recommend "Story of a Soul" by St. Therese of Lisieux, "Spiritual Exercises" by St. Ignatius of Loyola and "Come Be My Light" by Blessed Mother Teresa of Calcutta.

By reading about the life of saints, we see that there are many ways to engage in prayer. If we're attracted to a certain prayer style, we should try it. If we're not attracted to it, we should try it too! Praying to understand how to pray this way is a prayer in itself. It is often in our discomfort that we grow. What is most important about our prayer is that it is from the heart. It's about quality, not quantity, which can be difficult because some days it seems easier to say a lot of prayers, but not pray. Our Lady says in many of her messages to pray with the heart. She wants us to have a closer relationship with God. "Dear children! I invite you to pray with the heart in order that your prayer may be a conversation with God. I desire each one of you to dedicate more time to God" (September 25, 1990).

Our prayer schedule is not meant to confine us or to be a checklist. It is meant to free us and bring us closer to God. God doesn't want us babbling a bunch of words. God wants us. He wants us to trust him. He wants us to be his friend. That is what prayer is all about — learning to be friends with God. It's a relationship. That is what Our Lady of Medjugorje wants for us too. That is why she says: "Dear children! Today I invite you all so that your prayer will be prayer with the heart. Let each of you find time for prayer so that in prayer you discover God. I do not desire you to talk about prayer, but to pray. Let your everyday be filled with prayer of gratitude to God for life and for all that you have. I do not desire your life to pass by in words but that you glorify God with deeds. I am with you, and I am grateful to God for every moment spent with you. Thank you for having responded to my call" (April 25, 1991).

I'd like to address just one more point related to prayer: times when we don't think we have enough time to pray. There's a beautiful story about St. Mother Teresa of Calcutta who was asked what the community should do when they don't have enough time for one Holy Hour (in Adoration) with Jesus each day. Her response was profound, make *two* Holy Hours. I have found this to be true time and again. When we find ourselves not having time to pray is when we need to pray more. When we make that effort to pray even though we don't feel like we have time, we're telling God, "You are first, no matter what." God is delighted by such acts of love and I can share that there has *never* been a time after taking the time to pray when I said, "Oh I really shouldn't have done that."

I'm always amazed what happens afterward, because I end up having plenty of time, getting more done than I hoped, and most importantly, I have peace.

I wish I could include all the messages in which Our Lady speaks about prayer, but it'd be a book in itself. The essence of her messages about prayer reminds us that her Son Jesus is a real living person and prayer is our relationship with Him.

"Continue steadfastly in prayer" (Colossians 4:2).

Questions for Your Personal Reflection
1. Do I make time for silence in my heart to listen and to speak with God every day?
2. What is keeping me from wanting to pray and let God into those dark parts of my heart that need healing?
3. Have I been praying with my heart?

Questions for Small Group Discussion
1. What have been my most powerful encounters with Jesus while praying with Scripture?
2. When do I know that I'm praying with my heart?
3. What has surprised me about prayer?
4. Have I found that passage that I can go back to again and again?

Action Item
Read "Meditation and Contemplation: An Ignatian Guide to Praying with Scripture" by Fr. Timothy M. Gallagher, O.M.V.

Where's home?

Chapter 8

I used to think of heaven as somewhere far away, mysterious and unimaginable. I have since learned otherwise. Throughout my faith journey, I have learned to meditate and ponder the mysteries of heaven. Why? Because the journey began by meditating on the fact that I'm going to die. This is a truth we all have to confront. We are all going to die. At some point in our journey, we will be open to explore this truth. We recognize that we're pilgrims on earth and that heaven is our homeland. We will want to know more about what happens when we die, and what the church teaches about heaven, hell and purgatory. Most importantly, we will want to know how to prepare. This is a natural progression because we have decided to live intentionally for a reason, and that reason is heaven.

I'd like to take you on a journey to heaven, now.

You are on your deathbed. The priest has already come to hear your confession, given you the Anointing of the Sick and your final Holy Communion. Your loved ones are around your bedside praying the Divine Mercy Chaplet. While you may be in pain, there's a lightness growing in your heart. With each prayer, you seem to sense a closeness of Jesus and Mary. Your breathing becomes shallow and you start to slip out of consciousness. The voices of your loved ones fade away and you start to hear the faintness of a choir. In that moment, you see your guardian angel at your side and Our Lady. They are praying for you. St. Joseph is also present at the foot of your bed praying for you. Your body breathes its last, and all time seems to stop. You hear a most beautiful voice ask you only one question, "How did you love?" In that moment, you see your whole life before you. All your decisions: good and bad, holy and unholy. There's a clarity in your soul like you've never had. You trust Jesus and respond to the question, "As best I could, but I know I fell short, so that is why I trust in your mercy."

Your spirit is taken upwards and you see your body below still surrounded by loved ones. Your guardian angel is smiling at you and guiding you higher and higher still. The singing of a distant choir gets louder. The brightness of the light all around is brighter than a summer's day on earth. You reach the gates of heaven. They are beautiful, shiny and huge. There, St. Peter waits for you. He holds the keys in his hands and goes to open the door as he says over his shoulder with a smile, "We've been expecting you." The doors open and you see the streets of gold that are like glass (Revelation 21:21b). Not only that, but this path in front of you is lined with thousands of people. No, hundreds of thousands. They are there for you. They are cheering for you and singing. At the very end you see the brightest light.

Our Lady, just off to the right waves for you to come and meet her. As you look at your heavenly mother, up close, you are overwhelmed with love. You hug her and she kisses you on the forehead and says, "My child!" An angel brings her a tray with a garment neatly folded on it. Our Lady picks it up and says, "This is for you to wear." It is the most beautiful outfit: your favorite color, with your favorite accents, and as Our Lady slides it over your head, it fits perfectly. Another angel comes to Our Lady holding a tray with flowers. Our Lady takes each flower and carefully arranges them into a bouquet. As she's doing this, you understand that there is something significant about these flowers. She says, "These flowers are all the beautiful works you did while on earth. Being consecrated to me, you gave me the gift of collecting them and now arranging them into a bouquet. You will present them to my Son." At that, she gives you the bouquet. The aroma is overwhelmingly beautiful. Our Lady gives you another kiss and holds your cheeks in her hands, "You are ready to see Him!" She starts to lead you down the crowd-lined path. Everyone seems to know her and love her.

Your guardian angel nudges you to move forward and follow her. As you do, you see everyone waving and smiling and reaching out to touch your hand. As you look at the crowds, you realize you have a new knowledge. Just by looking at people, you understand that you prayed for them! They are in heaven because of your intercessory prayers. They say thank you with their smiles. You also look at other people and understand that they are the ones that prayed for you! You spot your grandfather and run to hug him. He looks wonderful — radiant, joyful and young. You want to stay and talk with him, but he says, "Keep going! Keep going!"

As you continue down the path, the choir gets louder and louder. The music is unlike anything you've heard. The light you're walking toward is getting brighter. You are drawn to its warmth and love. You see more family members, friends and neighbors in the crowd, and then St. Pio, St. Therese, St. Anthony — they are all there. You notice there are more angels too.

Our Lady looks back to you and reaches out her hand. Your guardian angel, still at your side, is nearly jumping for joy. You take Our Lady's hand and you approach the source of the light. At last the light takes a form — The Lamb of God, Jesus Christ. Our Lady kneels before him and you do likewise. She says, "Son, here is my child." You look up and Jesus is reaching down to give you his hand to help you up. You get to your feet, but melt in his embrace. There is only love. He wipes every tear from your eye. Everything in you is complete. You give him the bouquet of flowers. He accepts them with such tenderness and takes the time to smell them. He hugs you and says, "Well done, good and faithful servant ... Come, share your master's joy" (Matthew 25:23). At that, Jesus takes you to meet God the Father.

Heaven is real. And we get to choose it. Our seemingly "small" daily choices on earth have an eternal impact. With each choice, we live for heaven or for hell. We don't have to wait to die in order to begin living heaven. We are living in the eternal now. Heaven, hell and purgatory exist now. We can live it in our hearts, now. St. Therese of Lisieux said, "Our Lord does not come down from heaven every day to lie in a golden ciborium. He comes to find another heaven which is infinitely dearer to him — the heaven of our souls, created in his image, the living temples of the adorable Trinity."

While the above description is what I experienced in my meditation of heaven, I know it does not even capture the beauty, love and glory that await us. Perhaps in your own meditation, you experienced different details of heaven. St. Faustina described it:

> Today I was in heaven, in spirit, and I saw its inconceivable beauties and the happiness that awaits us after death. I saw how all creatures give ceaseless praise and glory to God. I saw how great is happiness in God, which spreads to all creatures, making them happy; and then all the glory and praise which springs from this happiness returns to its source; and they enter into the depths of God, contemplating the inner life of God, the Father, the Son, and the Holy Spirit, whom they will never comprehend or fathom. This source of happiness is unchanging in its essence, but it is always new, gushing forth happiness for all creatures.[11]

Contemplating heaven is part of our faith journey and we need to be reminded what we're choosing to live for, for all eternity. Jesus tells us, "Do not store up for yourselves treasures on earth, where moth and decay destroy, and thieves break in and steal. But store up treasures in heaven, where neither moth nor decay destroys, nor thieves break in and steal. For where your treasure is, there also will your heart be" (Matthew 6:19-21). Are our hearts in heaven? Are we storing up for heaven?

---

[11] Saint Faustina, Diary of Saint Maria Faustina Kowalska: Divine Mercy in My Soul (Stockbridge, MA: Marian Press, 2005), 310-311.

There's no doubt how easy it is to get distracted by this world and the things of this world. We live in a culture that has not only pushed out God, but has also forgotten heaven. We need to be reminded of heaven, and often. Many times, when we attend funerals, we are stirred to reflect on our own death. This is a grace from God. As a good father, he is reminding us that we are dust and unto dust we will return (Genesis 3:19). I don't think it was a coincidence that I learned about Medjugorje for the first time at the luncheon after a funeral. Only God knows that this funeral of my cousin and second cousin touched me deeply, weighed heavy on my heart, and inspired me to seek him in prayer. Death is part of life, but it is not the end. Jesus proves this by his Cross and Resurrection.

I have learned most about heaven through Our Lady of Medjugorje and her messages. These messages below speak of heaven, and I cannot help but share them because they teach and inspire me to live for heaven. I hope and pray they are also of help to you.

November 27, 1986
"Dear children! Again today I call you to consecrate your life to me with love, so I am able to guide you with love. I love you, dear children, with a special love, and I desire to bring you all to heaven unto God. I want you to realize that this life lasts briefly compared with the one in heaven. Therefore, dear children, decide again today for God. Only in that way will I be able to show how much you are dear to me and how much I desire all to be saved and to be with me in heaven. Thank you for having responded to my call."

July 25, 1987
"Dear children! I beseech you to take up the way of holiness beginning today. I love you and, therefore, I want you to be holy. I do not want Satan to block you on that way. Dear children, pray and accept all that God is offering you in a way which is bitter. But at the same time, God will reveal every sweetness to whoever begins to go on that way, and that person will gladly answer every call of God. Do not attribute

importance to petty things. Long for heaven. Thank you for having responded to my call."

February 25, 1988
"Dear children! Today again I am calling you to prayer to complete surrender to God. You know that I love you and am coming here out of love so I could show you the path to peace and salvation for your souls. I want you to obey me and not permit Satan to seduce you. Dear children, Satan is very strong and, therefore, I ask you to dedicate your prayers to me so that those who are under his influence can be saved. Give witness by your life. Sacrifice your lives for the salvation of the world. I am with you, and I am grateful to you, but in heaven you shall receive the Father's reward which he has promised to you. Therefore, dear children, do not be afraid. If you pray, Satan cannot injure you even a little bit because you are God's children, and he is watching over you. Pray and let the rosary always be in your hand as a sign to Satan that you belong to me. Thank you for having responded to my call."

August 25, 1990
"Dear children! I desire to invite you to take with seriousness and put into practice the messages, which I am giving you. You know, little children, that I am with you, and I desire to lead you along the same path to heaven, which is beautiful for those who discover it in prayer. Therefore, little children, do not forget that those messages which I am giving you have to be put into your everyday life in order that you might be able to say: 'There, I have taken the messages and tried to live them.' Dear children, I am protecting you before the heavenly Father by my own prayers. Thank you for having responded to my call."

May 25, 1991
"Dear Children! Today I invite all of you who have heard my message of peace to realize it with seriousness and with love in your life. There are many who think that they are doing a lot by talking about the messages, but who do not live them. Dear children, I invite you to life and to change all that is negative in you, so that it all turns into the

positive and life. Dear children, I am with you, and I desire to help each of you to live and by living, to witness the good news. I am here, dear children, to help you and to lead you to heaven, and heaven is the joy, which you can already live now. Thank you for having responded to my call!"

May 25, 1996
"Dear children! Today I wish to thank you for all your prayers and sacrifices that you, during this month, which is consecrated to me, have offered to me. Little children, I also wish that you all become active during this time that through me is connected to heaven in a special way. Pray in order to understand that you all, through your life and your example, ought to collaborate in the work of salvation. Little children, I wish that all people convert and see me and my son Jesus in you. I will intercede for you and help you to become the light. In helping others, your soul will also find salvation. Thank you for having responded to my call."

May 25, 1997
"Dear children! Today I invite you to glorify God and for the Name of God to be holy in your hearts and in your life. Little children, when you are in the holiness of God, he is with you and gives you peace and joy, which come from God only through prayer. That is why, little children, renew prayer in your families, and your heart will glorify the Holy Name of God, and heaven will reign in your heart. I am close to you, and I intercede for you before God. Thank you for having responded to my call."

July 25, 2000
"Dear children! Do not forget that you are here on earth on the way to eternity and that your home is in heaven. That is why, little children, be open to God's love and leave egoism and sin behind. May your joy be only in discovering God in daily prayer. That is why, make good use of this time and pray, pray, pray; for God is near to you in prayer and through prayer. Thank you for having responded to my call."

April 25, 2011

"Dear children! As nature gives the most beautiful colors of the year, I also call you to witness with your life and to help others to draw closer to my Immaculate Heart, so that the flame of love for the Most High may sprout in their hearts. I am with you, and I unceasingly pray for you that your life may be a reflection of heaven here on earth. Thank you for having responded to my call."

February 2, 2012

"Dear children, I am with you for so much time, and already for so long I have been pointing you to God's presence and his infinite love, which I desire for all of you to come to know. And you, my children? You continue to be deaf and blind as you look at the world around you and do not want to see where it is going without my Son. You are renouncing him, and he is the source of all graces. You listen to me while I am speaking to you, but your hearts are closed, and you are not hearing me. You are not praying to the Holy Spirit to illuminate you. My children, pride has come to rule. I am pointing out humility to you. My children, remember that only a humble soul shines with purity and beauty, because it has come to know the love of God. Only a humble soul goes to heaven, because my Son is in it. Thank you. Again I implore you to pray for those whom my Son has chosen; those are your shepherds."

June 02, 2012

"Dear children, I am continuously among you because, with my endless love I desire to show you the door of heaven. I desire to tell you how it is opened: through goodness, mercy, love and peace, through my son. Therefore, my children, do not waste time on vanities. Only knowledge of the love of my son can save you. Through that salvific love and the Holy Spirit se chose me and I, together with him, am choosing you to be apostles of his love and will. My children, great is the responsibility upon you. I desire that by your example you help sinners regain their sight, enrich their poor souls, and bring them back into my embrace. Therefore, pray, pray, fast, and confess regularly. If receiving my son in the Eucharist is the center of your life, then do not be afraid; you can do everything. I am with you. Every day I pray for the shepherds, and I expect the same of you, because, my children, without their guidance and strengthening through their blessing, you cannot do it. Thank you."

May 02, 2014

"Dear children, I, your mother, am with you for the sake of your well-being, for the sake of your needs and for the sake of your personal cognition. The Heavenly Father gave you the freedom to decide on your own and to become cognizant on your own. I desire to help you. I desire to be a mother to you, a teacher of the truth — so that in the simplicity of an open heart, you may become cognizant of the immeasurable purity and light which comes from it and shatters darkness, the light which brings hope. I, my children, understand your pain and suffering. Who could understand you better than a mother? And you, my children? Small is the number of those who understand and follow me. Great is the number of those who are lost — of those who have not yet become cognizant of the truth in my son. Therefore, my apostles, pray and act. Bring the light and do not lose hope. I am with you. In a special way I am with your shepherds. With a motherly heart I love and protect them, because they lead you to heaven that was promised to you by my son. Thank you."[12]

"Blessed are the poor in spirit, for theirs is the kingdom of heaven." (Matthew 5:3)

Questions for Your Personal Reflection

1. What will I do when I see Jesus face to face?
2. Whom do I hope to see in heaven?
3. How can I make time to meditate on heaven? What will my reflections say about how much I have loved in my life? How can I make changes to love more?

---

[12] "Concordance of Our Lady's Messages 1981-2014," Medjugorje Web, accessed 2 June, 2016. <https://www.medjugorje.org/concordance/framconc.htm>

Questions for Small Group Discussion

1. What changes am I inspired to make after meditating on heaven?
2. How often do I meditate on heaven? What snippets do I find myself going back to?
3. How can I make heaven more of a reality for me and my loved ones?

Action Item

Meditate on the details of heaven and write it down.

Another Nazareth

I had originally titled this chapter "Sacramentals," but as I was writing it, I realized how it's really about making your home another Nazareth where Jesus and Mary can dwell.

Sacramentals are blessed holy objects. Back in the day, sacramentals were widely used and respected. It is no wonder, then, that with the decline of the knowledge of Satan, there has also been a decline in the use of sacramentals to repel him. They can include holy water, candles, rosaries, medals, and Bibles. Mother Church gave us sacramentals to lead us to the sacraments. Every time we bless ourselves with holy water, we reaffirm our baptismal promises. Blessed medals and rosaries encourage us to pray. Our Lady reminds us of the importance of blessed objects in one of her messages, "Dear children! Today I call you to place more blessed objects in your homes and that everyone put some blessed objects on their person. Bless all the objects, and thus Satan will attack you less because you will have armor against him. Thank you for having responded to my call" (July 18, 1985).

We need to have our homes blessed. It used to be a widely common practice and still is in some countries. The priest blesses homes throughout town on or after the Epiphany. We need to get back into that habit. Especially here in the United States. It's amazing that before purchasing a house, we go through all the physical inspections. We hire inspectors and then contractors to fix anything that didn't pass. But then we often neglect the spiritual side. The naked eye cannot see what was done in that house and who lived there years before. Or what was done on that land. A home blessing addresses these issues and it's free.

A priest's blessing is that of Jesus. It dispels evil and the Lord's blessing remains. Wouldn't you want Jesus to walk through your house and bless it?

I remember when the priest came to bless our first apartment. The place was no more than 900 square feet. Father Andrew brought his book of blessings and holy water. He took it very seriously and opened every closet. There was a crawl space under the stairs and he got on his hands and knees to be sure to get holy water in there. We cannot underestimate the power of holy water. It's important to have holy water in your home and to use it. In our family, we bless ourselves with holy water each morning, and it's a wonderful opportunity to continue teaching our daughter how to bless herself. It's also good to have blessed salt. Especially in the dry months when the water dries up quickly in the font, you can have blessed salt instead. Holy water and blessed salt are called such because of the blessing by a priest. Most churches have a holy water dispenser where you can bring your own container to fill and bring home. If you want blessed salt, you will probably have to bring the salt and ask the priest to bless it. There's a difference between a normal blessing (sign of the cross) over salt and water, and the exorcised blessing that comes from the *Roman Ritual*. If possible, get the exorcised water and salt.

Blessed crucifixes also belong in each home. (Religious objects like crucifixes, rosaries and medals should be blessed before use.) Especially above the beds where family members sleep. St. Angela Merici said, "Remember that the devil doesn't sleep, but seeks our ruin in a thousand ways." Yet we humans need our sleep. So having a blessed crucifix above us as we sleep signals being under the protection of the Cross of Jesus. It is also important for us to wear blessed crucifixes. For a long time, they used to be baptism gifts. Crucifixes are powerful. That is where Jesus defeated sin, death and Satan. The mystery of our salvation and God's love is found at the cross. Not only do crucifixes provide protection, but they also remind us of what Jesus did for us. Having them in the home and on us, we see them more often, and in difficult moments we can turn to Jesus more quickly.

While we're on the home blessing, we might as well do the Enthronement of the Sacred Heart. "It is a ceremony in which an image of the Sacred Heart is enthroned in a prominent place as a sign that Jesus is the King, friend and brother of the family. It is also an act of reparation for the widespread ignoring of Christ, the basic cause of the evils that today plague us."[13] My first enthronement was at the convent with Mother Olga's community. Msgr. Esseff led the ceremony and said that when Jesus is enthroned, then Satan is automatically dethroned. Jesus became the king of our hearts and our home. Our Lady of Medjugorje encourages us to consecrate ourselves too, "Dear children! Also today I urge you to consecrate yourselves to my Heart and to the Heart of my Son Jesus. Only in this way will you be mine more each day, and you will inspire each other all the more to holiness. In this way joy will rule your hearts, and you will be carriers of peace and love. Thank you for having responded to my call" (May 25, 2004).

Christian and I did the Enthronement of the Sacred Heart together for the first time as a married couple shortly after we moved into our apartment. The ceremony also included Holy Mass. One of the lines the family says is, "Jesus, we enthrone you as King and proclaim you as Lord and Friend of our (family). Yes Lord, we do want you to rule over our hearts and wills through your loving Heart. Share our everyday life; our joys and sorrows. Be our well-beloved Brother, our intimate Friend!" We have this Sacred Heart image on the fireplace mantle in our living room, though you may wish to have a more discreet location. The personal consecration and devotion to the Sacred Heart are the key here. It's a reminder that our home is another Nazareth. Jesus is with us. Words cannot describe the peace Jesus brings. For that is the most wonderful compliment our home ever received — "it's so peaceful." Amen. The presence of Jesus dwelling with us is noticeable. Sure

---

[13] "Sacred Heart of Jesus Home Enthronement," Buildingakingdomoflove.org, accessed 25 June, 2016. <http://www.msgrjohnesseff.net/?page_id=92>

you want to have a clean, bright, cheerful home to create, but peace comes from above. Jesus said, "Today I must stay at your house" (Luke 19:5). By enthroning him, we welcome him to stay with us. Msgr. Esseff has a website (www.buildingakingdomoflove.org) with resources for Enthroning the Sacred Heart. There's another resource, *Family Divine Mercy* (www.familydivinemercy.org), so families can consecrate themselves to Jesus, Divine Mercy.

Jesus revealed a number of promises to St. Margaret Mary Alacoque for those who practice a devotion to the Sacred Heart. Jesus promised that...

1. "I will give them all the graces necessary in their state of life."
2. "I will establish peace in their homes."
3. "I will comfort them in all their afflictions."
4. "I will be their secure refuge during life, and above all in death."
5. "I will bestow a large blessing upon all their undertakings."
6. "Sinners shall find in my heart the source and the infinite ocean of mercy."
7. "Tepid souls shall grow fervent."
8. "Fervent souls shall quickly mount to high perfection."
9. "I will bless every place where a picture of my Heart shall be set up and honored."
10. "I will give to priests the gifts of touching the most hardened hearts."
11. "Those who shall promote this devotion shall have their names written in my Heart, never to be effaced."
12. "I promise you in the excessive mercy of my Heart that my all-powerful love will grant to all those who communicate on the First Friday in nine consecutive months the grace of final penitence; they shall not die in my disgrace nor without receiving their sacraments; My divine Heart shall be their safe refuge in this last moment."[14]

---

[14] "The Promises of Our Lord to Saint Margaret Mary: For Souls Devoted to His Sacred Heart," EWTN, accessed 25 February, 2016. <https://www.ewtn.com/faith/teachings/incab2.htm>

I don't know about you, but I don't want to miss out on those powerful promises!

St. Benedict medals go back a number of years, but they are powerful because they are blessed with an exorcism prayer. The medal may be worn, placed about doorway entrances, or used with the St. Benedict crucifix.

You probably already have a Bible and rosaries, and maybe everything above, but it's worth mentioning. The Holy Bible is God's word and should be treated with the utmost respect. We are also encouraged to have it in a place of honor where we see it regularly, so we are more inclined to read it. God's word is living and true. It's powerful. It was by God's word that the world was created. We need to read, meditate and study the Word of God, so let's be sure to have a Bible in our home.

Onto the rosary. Back in April 2015, Catholic News Agency published an article about a vision a Nigerian Bishop had about the rosary. I'd like to share some of it with you:

"A Nigerian bishop says that he has seen Christ in a vision and now knows that the rosary is the key to ridding the country of the Islamist terrorist organization Boko Haram. Bishop Oliver Dashe Doeme says he is being driven by a God-given mandate to lead others in praying the rosary until the extremist group disappears. "Towards the end of last year I was in my chapel before the Blessed Sacrament ... praying the rosary, and then suddenly the Lord appeared," Bishop Dashe told CNA April 18. In the vision, the prelate said that Jesus didn't say anything at first, but extended a sword toward him, and he in turn reached out for it.

"As soon as I received the sword, it turned into a rosary," the bishop said, adding that Jesus then told him three times: "Boko Haram is gone."

"I didn't need any prophet to give me the explanation," he said. "It was clear that with the rosary we would be able to expel Boko Haram." The bishop said he didn't want to tell anyone, but "felt that the Holy Spirit was pushing him to do so."[15]

The rosary is our weapon. Our Lady speaks of it that way in her messages too. Once she said, "Satan wants to work still more now that you know he is at work. Dear children, put on the armor for battle, and with the rosary in your hand defeat him!" (August 8, 1985). And then, "With the rosary you shall overcome all the adversities which Satan is trying to inflict on the Catholic Church" (June 25, 1985). When we have rosaries in our home, we are more likely to make a commitment to pray it. Our Lady reminds us though, "The rosary is not an ornament for the home, as one often time-limits himself to using it. Tell everyone to pray it" (March 18,1985).

The rosary is a beautiful prayer because we meditate on the life events of Jesus and Mary. We draw closer to them. In the early morning hours on the day our second daughter was born, I was praying the rosary and Our Lady inspired something new to me during each mystery. I want to share with you what I learned in the fifth Joyful mystery — the finding of Jesus in the temple. When Joseph and Mary found Jesus after searching for him for three days and Mary asked him why he did this to them, Jesus responded, "Why were you looking for me? Did you not know that I must be in my Father's house?" (Luke 2:49). Scripture goes on to say, "But they did not understand what he said to them . . . and his mother kept all these things in her heart" (Luke 2:50-51). As I was pondering this with Our Lady, she taught me that Jesus was indicating his future dwelling in the temple — in the Eucharist. "Did you not know that I must be in my Father's house?" now had a whole new meaning. Since Mother Mary stored all these things in her heart, she can share them with us in prayer.

---

[15] CNA/EWTN News, "After vision of Christ, Nigerian bishop says rosary will bring down Boko Haram" Catholic News Agency, last modified 21 April, 2015.
<http://www.catholicnewsagency.com/news/after-vision-of-christ-nigerian-bishop-says-rosary-will-bring-down-boko-haram-78382/>

In one of her more recent messages she said, "And to me, my children, give the gift of the rosary, the roses which I love so much. My roses are your prayers pronounced with the heart and not only recited with the lips. My roses are your acts of prayer, faith and love. When my Son was little, he said to me that my children would be numerous and that they would bring me many roses. I did not comprehend Him. Now I know that you are those children who are bringing me roses when, above all, you love my Son, when you pray with the heart, when you help the poorest. Those are my roses" (December 2, 2017).

On my first trip to Medjugorje, I was given a Catholic prayer book. This is something I refer to often and where I continue to learn new prayers. Such prayer books usually divide prayers by category/topic, which can be very helpful in all sorts of circumstances. Just by looking through the book, we may find that we want to say certain prayers each day, like for priests, the Pope, or the unborn. Sometimes we seem to have so many intentions and don't know where to start. Well, there's a "Prayer for many intentions." A liturgical calendar ties in beautifully with this point because, just as the Church has prayers for us in all circumstances, the Church's calendar also leads us through the various seasons of the year. I would recommend a liturgical calendar that also includes the saint of the day. In this way you can ask for his or her intercession and make the time to look up a little about his or her life. The calendar reminds us that there are Solemnities and Feast Days to be celebrated, as well as days of mourning and penance. Awareness of the liturgical calendar better prepares us for Holy Mass, and in a profound way unites us to the universal Church.

Lastly, every home needs an image of Our Lady. She is our Mother and intercedes for us in a powerful way. More on Our Lady to come in another chapter, but having her image in our home reminds us to be childlike, trusting in God, pure in body and mind, courageous, obedient, faithful, tender, loving and humble. We need her presence too. Find an image of Our Lady that really speaks to your heart — one that inspires you to ponder the divine, such as "The Innocence," "The Madonna," or a more recent one. Again, put her in a place of honor and somewhere you will see her regularly. She will help you pray more and draw you closer to her son, Jesus.

In summary, here are some items you might wish to have in your home to help you continue growing in your faith:

- Crucifixes in rooms
- Holy Water and salt in fonts or individual containers
- St. Benedict medals
- Sacred Heart image for the Enthronement (in a frame of honor)
- Holy Bible
- Rosaries
- Prayer book
- Liturgical calendar
- Our Lady image

"Behold, I stand at the door and knock (Revelation 3:20).

Questions for Your Personal Reflection

1. Do I have a Holy Bible in my home? Is it somewhere where I readily access it?
2. What from this chapter speaks to me about how to make my home more holy?

Questions for Small Group Discussion

1. Have I noticed a change since the home blessings and enthronement?
2. Why has it been helpful having a holy image to glance at?
3. What are some ways I've made using Holy Water a habit?

Action Item

Organize a home blessing and Enthrone the Sacred Heart of Jesus— invite your friends from the small group.

Your best friends

Chapter 10

We forget that being in the Body of Christ, we are connected to the saints and angels. The saints and angels pray for us and intercede for us every day. They want to help us and they want us to ask for their help. Again, it was in Medjugorje that my spiritual eyes were opened and I learned about these heavenly friends.

Growing in devotion to the angels and saints has a two-fold blessing. First, we learn more about them — the who, what, where, when, why and how. As we do, we learn more about God and our faith. Seeking such knowledge is always a blessing in our faith journey because we are active. The Lord says, "Ask and it will be given to you; seek and you will find; knock and the door will be opened to you" (Matthew 7:7). We will be given what we seek. Second, we gain intercessors. We can call upon the angels and saints by name to help us in our needs. We can start to have relationships with them. St. Therese of Lisieux is known to give roses at the end of novenas prayed for her intercession. The saints are part of God's family and he wants us to see them as ours too. Our Lady also encourages us to imitate the lives of the saints in a handful of her messages: "I invite you to open yourselves and to live, taking the saints as an example. Mother Church has chosen them, that they may be an impulse for your daily life" (October 25, 1994). We receive more graces by being in relationships with the angels and saints, which leads us into a deeper union with God.

We can forget that we have a guardian angel whom God assigned to us from our conception until our death. This guardian angel is a dear companion and he always sees the face of God. He not only intercedes for our spiritual needs, but also for our temporal needs. This angel never leaves our side, nor does he accompany any other human. His task is to help you, and you only, get to heaven. "Oh, if all men could understand this great gift that God assigned to us; this celestial spirit" (St. Padre Pio).

St. Padre Pio was blessed in that he was given the grace to see and interact with his guardian angel from a very young age. When he became a priest, and people would want to visit him, he'd often tell them to send their guardian angel instead. St. Padre Pio teaches us to have a close relationship with our guardian angel, to call upon him often and to put him to work. He said, "Invoke your guardian angel that he will illuminate you and will guide you. God has given him to you for this reason. Therefore use him!"

Sometimes this simple reminder of our heavenly companion can spark a new fire in our souls. Becoming aware of his presence, we are also becoming aware of God's love. Why not tell our guardian angel what we're struggling with? Why not confide in him our misery and ask him to help us? If we get distracted during Mass, could we not call upon his intercession to keep our hearts and minds attentive and actively participating? As we grow in awareness and devotion to our guardian angel, we lift our hearts to God more readily and more frequently throughout the day. We end up praying more.

A beautiful prayer we can learn is the following:

Angel of God, my guardian dear
to whom his love commits me here.
Ever this day (or night) be at my side
to light and guard, to rule and guide.
Amen.

We can learn most about angels in Scripture, as well as from the lives of saints. The first reference to an angel in the Bible is in the book of

Genesis, after Adam and Eve leave the Garden of Eden. "He expelled the man, stationing the cherubim and the fiery revolving sword east of the Garden of Eden, to guard the way to the tree of life" (Genesis 3:24). Here we see that God uses an angel, specifically a cherubim, to guard the way to the tree of life. This passage beautifully complements St. Faustina's account of her guardian angel and angels stationed at Catholic churches:

> Then I saw one of the seven spirits near me, radiant as at other times, under a form of light. I constantly saw him beside me when I was riding on the train. I saw an angel standing on every church we passed, but surrounded by a light which was paler than that of the spirit who was accompanying me on the journey, and each of these spirits who were guarding the churches bowed his head to the spirit who was near me . . . I thanked God for his goodness, that he gives us angels for companions. Oh, how little people reflect on the fact that they always have beside them such a guest, and at the same time a witness to everything! Remember, sinners, that you likewise have a witness to all your deeds.[16]

In both Genesis and St. Faustina's account, we learn that God has stationed angels throughout the earth as guardians. We also read how angels helped the prophets Isaiah, Ezekiel, Daniel and Zechariah, and that they often came in disguise as humans. "Do not neglect hospitality, for through it some have unknowingly entertained angels" (Hebrews 13:2).

The angels mentioned by name in Scripture include Raphael (Tobit 12:15) known as the healer, Michael (Daniel 10:13) known as the defender, and Gabriel (Daniel 8:16, Luke 1:19) known as the messenger. St. Raphael, St. Michael and St. Gabriel are archangels. The Catholic

---

16 Saint Faustina, *Diary of Saint Maria Faustina Kowalska: Divine Mercy in My Soul* (Stockbridge, MA: Marian Press, 2005), 262-263.

Church teaches that there are nine Choirs of Angels — seraphim, cherubim, thrones, dominions, virtues, powers, principalities, archangels and angels.

We see that angels were also part of Jesus' life, beginning with the Annunciation when Gabriel brought the message to Mary that, "Behold, you will conceive in your womb and bear a son, and you shall name him Jesus. He will be great and will be called Son of the Most High, and the Lord God will give him the throne of David his father, and he will rule over the house of Jacob forever, and of his kingdom there will be no end" (Luke 1:31-33). We see them again at Jesus' birth, when an angel announces to the shepherds that the Messiah has been born (Luke 2:9-11). In fact, it seems that heaven cannot contain the joy and praise for what happens next, "And suddenly there was a multitude of the heavenly host with the angel, praising God and saying: 'Glory to God in the highest and on earth peace to those on whom his favor rests' " (Luke 2:13-14). We join the angels in this praise every time we go to Mass.

The Gospel accounts of Jesus' encounters with angels during his adulthood emphasize their presence during times of great trial and tribulation. For example, at the end of Jesus' temptations in the desert for 40 days, Matthew recounts, "Then the devil left him and, behold, angels came and ministered to him" (Matthew 4:11). An angel also ministered to Jesus in the Garden of Gethsemane, "After withdrawing about a stone's throw from them and kneeling, he prayed, saying, 'Father, if you are willing, take this cup away from me; still, not my will but yours be done.' And to strengthen him an angel from heaven appeared to him" (Luke 22: 41-43). We can ask Jesus, How did the angels minister to you? What did they say or do? The angels were part of Jesus' life, as he said to his disciples, "Amen, amen, I say to you, you will see the sky opened and the angels of God ascending and descending on the Son of Man" (John 1:51). He wants them to be part of our lives too.

Even Jesus' apostles experience the workings of angels. For example, St. Peter was led out of prison by an angel (Acts 12). Then we can go to the book of Revelation and see how angels are ministers of God's plans. These examples are just glimpses, but it goes to show that there is much to be learned about angels. To say angels aren't for us is to ignore a part of who we are as children of God. Exploring this aspect of our faith is essential to our faith journey because we learn that we're not alone, that God blesses us, and that there is much more to our lives than what we can see with our eyes. On August 2, 2005, Our Lady said, "Dear children, I came to you with open arms, so that I could take you all into my arms, under my mantle. I cannot do this while your hearts are filled with false light and false idols. Cleanse them, and let my angels sing in them. Then I will take you under my mantle and give you my son, true peace, and happiness. Do not wait, my children. Thank you!"

Saints are in heaven with God, yet we forget we're in communion with them just by being part of the Body of Christ. The saints know how to love God and they can teach us how to love God more. Their lives glorified God while they lived on earth, but also now as they praise him in heaven. We can learn so much by reading about them and praying with them. Their stories are like our stories. We can see ourselves in them: their struggles, temptations, situations, prayers and blessings. We can see how God worked in their lives and how he used them as instruments. We can see how God has a specific plan for our life, and while there are billions of us, he wants a personal relationship with each of us.

We can begin on our journey to better know the angels and saints by reading about the Saint of the Day, or when we are struggling with a certain issue or predicament, we can look up the patron saint for it. By asking for his/her intercession, we are again raising our hearts and minds to God. We are praying. Maybe we can learn a prayer that one of the saints wrote or maybe we can read their autobiography. Saints also have a way of making their way into our lives. Maybe it's a prayer card of a saint given to you, or a medal or book. Let us have open hearts to accept these invitations to befriend our heavenly brothers and sisters.

My experience with angels and saints has been extraordinary and continues to be. A few Sunday evenings ago, my husband and I were looking at our week ahead. Something about an activity we had planned for our children made me nervous. (I have to be vague about this story.) There was nothing about it that I could put my finger on, but something within me said, "Don't do it." I tried to dismiss it, thinking I was maybe overreacting, but the restlessness was troubling. The activity was one that would be awkward and challenging to get out of, and would impact my work schedule, so my pragmatic side said, "let it go, everything is fine." But, I did not have peace. I expressed it to my husband, who was also unsure about pursuing an investigation, but he has learned to trust these instincts. He suggested we make a call to a trusted spiritual adviser.

Within 10 minutes we had our answer. The spiritual adviser called back and validated my instinct. She not only told me it was good to act on my concerns, but confirmed specific facets of my uncertainty about the situation. She said, "Your husband and your children are your priority. Learn from this experience and pray for discernment of spirits daily." I was overcome with emotion. My instinct was confirmed. It was shocking and a relief at the same time. We started thanking God right away for protecting our family. We canceled that activity immediately.

Once the emotions of it settled down, I reflected on how it must have been my guardian angel's protective intercession. From the restlessness I felt to the actual "don't do it." Our angels are constantly at work for our good. They protect us, guide us and intercede for us.

Perhaps you've had a similar encounter or perhaps not. Perhaps you haven't explored what the Church teaches about these celestial beings. Either way, the angels and saints are part of our lives and they will be present in our life to come. We can and should get to know them now. As Our Lady suggests, "Dear children! Today, on the day of the patron of your parish, I call you to imitate the lives of the saints. May they be, for you, an example and encouragement to a life of holiness. May prayer for you be like the air you breathe in and not a burden. Little children, God will reveal his love to you, and you will experience the joy that you are my beloved. God will bless you and give you an abundance of grace. Thank you for having responded to my call" (July 25, 2007).

"For he commands his angels with regard to you, to guard you wherever you go" (Psalm 91:11).

Questions for Your Personal Reflection
1. How will I start praying to my guardian angel more intentionally?
2. What saint have I been inspired to learn about?
3. How can I better prepare myself to experience the reality of angels in my life? What do I need to do to listen better to God's voice?

Questions for Small Group Discussion
1. What saint has made a distinct presence in my life and what have I learned from him or her?
2. Reflecting on my life, can I think of a time when I had seemingly heavenly help, perhaps from my guardian angel?
3. What have I noticed since praying to my guardian angel daily?

Action Item
Each group member chooses a saint to research and learn more about, and then each person presents about his/her saint at the next gathering.

I'm sorry

Chapter 11

This is a chapter you might be inclined to skip over, but don't. We all need to say, "I'm sorry" to someone. We humans are funny beings because deep down we all think we're right. We tend to take suggestions only from people who agree with us, and when we're wrong, we think we're not *that* wrong. It's no wonder that when we lived in sin, we surrounded ourselves with others doing the same. To admit we were wrong takes courage. It starts with admitting it to God and that's what confession is all about. But what about those people you hurt along the way? Either intentionally or unintentionally — we have all done it. This chapter is about apologizing and reconciling with those we've hurt. I know I've hurt family, friends and even strangers along the way, especially in my earlier years, and I ask for your forgiveness. I'm sorry if I didn't treat you with respect and if I caused you any suffering. Please, please forgive me.

Apologizing isn't easy. We are asking another person to accept our apology and to give us mercy for the wrong we did. While we may have a good and pure intention to reconcile, we must be prepared that the person might not want to forgive us. That's okay, pray for them. You have done your part. I found that in-person apologies are the best, but also the hardest. Chances are, there will be many tears. When forgiveness is given and received, blessings flow. If an in-person apology isn't feasible due to distance or some other factor, then a phone call or a letter are other good options. In some ways, a letter often lets us open up and really get to the heart of the matter in a way that a conversation doesn't. It's because a letter lets us get everything out without any interruptions or changing our wording based on how well it is or isn't being received. You know what you need to apologize for. Now it shouldn't be a laundry list. There are probably specific incidences that come to mind and without going into great detail, address them. There are also perhaps more general behaviors that likewise necessitate asking for forgiveness. Remember to pray to the Holy Spirit to help you in this process. Oftentimes, he can help you see something in a new way and you can see the truth of the situation.

Now, just because you've spent this time preparing an apology and examining ways you've failed in this relationship, it doesn't mean that this person has to accept your apology. You hope and pray that they do, but they might not. If they do accept it, there is great reconciliation and peace is restored. There's a burst of grace in that relationship and a newness to it. If the person doesn't accept your apology, then you can't take it personally. Your role is then to pray for them.

The second part of seeking forgiveness is to forgive others for the wrong they've done to us. This tends to be overlooked, but we pray for this in the Our Father when we say, "Forgive us our trespasses as we forgive those who trespass against us." It's our human nature to want justification when we've been hurt. It's especially hard to forgive someone who hasn't apologized. You might say, "But don't I deserve an apology? Where's the justice in that?" We can learn from Jesus hanging on the cross. He didn't receive an apology, yet he said, "Father forgive them, they know not what they do." That is the beauty of mercy, especially Divine Mercy. It doesn't need an apology to act. It flows from the very depths of the Father's heart, and we are called to do the same: to forgive without conditions and without limits. St. Peter asked Jesus how many times we are required to forgive, seven? And Jesus says, "I say to you, not seven times but seventy-seven times" (Matthew 18:22).

Sometimes we think that by withholding forgiveness, we're getting even with a person. We have resentment towards him or her, and we spend energy on ways of not giving our respect. So while it may seem like we're doing something to the person, we're really doing it to ourselves.

Maybe this is the only time we can ever say, "Be selfish," because you will be better off when you forgive. To forgive is to let go of judging that person in our heart and letting God judge them instead. Now it doesn't mean that every time we're offended by another we say or think, "God will judge you for that!" However we can acknowledge the hurt inflicted on us and choose not to judge the person by it. We hand it over to God and ask him to be merciful. Remember, we will receive the forgiveness that we give: "If you forgive others their transgressions, your heavenly Father will forgive you. But if you do not forgive others, neither will your Father forgive your transgressions" (Matthew 6:14-15).

Forgiveness is really a key to the virtue of trust. Forgiveness cuts off the strings and allows us to take a new step in trust. From my own observations, I have noticed that those who are the most forgiving are the most trusting in God. Forgiveness is something we will work on the rest of our lives and it is essential to our faith journey. Our Lady speaks many times about forgiveness throughout her messages. "There is no love without prayer — there is no prayer without forgiveness because love is prayer — forgiveness is love. My children, God created you to love and you love so as to forgive" (June 02, 2014). To forgive is to love.

We can ask God now for the grace to forgive anyone who has hurt us in our past — whether physical, spiritual, emotional, mental or psychological. There are two people that everyone can forgive and it's so obvious that you might say, "Really?" They are our mother and father. We all have them. Whether we had good or bad relationships, didn't know them or knew them well, we all, in one way or another, were hurt by our parents. As a parent now, this is a difficult truth to accept, but it is because of our sinfulness from original sin that we will inevitably hurt our children. Children will also hurt their parents. That is why asking for and giving forgiveness in the family is so important. It was only after I wrote this that I came across one of Our Lady's messages expressing the importance of forgiveness in the family, "I am with you, and I invite all of you, little children, before all else to forgive in the family, and then you will be able to forgive others" (January 25, 1996).

As adults, we can be quick to say, "Oh, I know my parents did the best they could. I don't have anything to forgive them for." But if we really take the time to reflect — especially now that Jesus is your everything — when they, in their humanity, didn't fulfill their duty in bringing us closer to God and in some cases led us astray, we will find places where we haven't forgiven them. Whether their guilt is real or imagined, we want to forgive them, so as to let go of any resentment we may hold toward them.

Forgiveness is ongoing because there will be instances when we forgive someone, but then discover more details later on that seem to reopen the wound. We can wonder if we forgave the person in the first place, or if our forgiveness was lacking somehow. This is normal to experience. Now is when we need to forgive again. We need to forgive based on the new circumstances. Maybe we'll need to offer forgiveness in our heart every time we see the person. Forgiveness is a choice, and we need to make that choice again and again and again. It's like getting annoying spam email. We need to flag it right when it comes into our mailbox (mind). We need to acknowledge it as spam and delete it right away. The subject might even be captivating, "Maybe if I had said that differently ..." but don't click. Don't open that spam email. Even if we're curious. Don't open up to replaying the incident in our mind. Just like computers, we will get a virus — the virus of unforgiveness, and it will eat away at everything else in us. The better we get at recognizing the spam email, the better we can let forgiveness grow in us.

Learning to have a forgiving heart takes humility because it invites us to look outside of ourselves, and the way we see something with our filters. For example, we can say hello to a cashier and the person doesn't respond. We take offense and move on. Yet, as we learn to have a forgiving heart, we move past ourselves, knowing that everyone is fighting his or her own battles and then this becomes our filter. Instead of having a heart ready to be offended, we can have a heart ready to be compassionate. We can turn those prime areas of our hearts susceptible to offense into areas of offering a prayer for the offender.

I'm sure my husband won't mind my sharing that he can get pretty frustrated driving on the roads of Boston. (I think a lot of Boston drivers can relate!) When he throws his hands in the air, I know he's had it. Granted, he is justified in his anger because someone just came across three lanes without a blinker and cut him off so that he could be four inches closer to the light. Unnecessary, yes. In these situations, I will chime in, "Maybe they're trying to get to the hospital to see a dying relative. Let's pray for them." So there we are saying three hail Marys for this driver. We each have something we're more prone to be offended by. Bad drivers aren't mine, which is why I can say what I say to my husband and mean it. We each have something. Mine is when I'm sitting in a public space and there are lots of open seats around, but someone decides to sit right next me. That's precisely the thing, though — we don't know the full picture. We don't know exactly what others are going through or have been through. We don't know what their upbringing was like. We don't know the state of their souls. We don't know a lot, and that's why we need humility to live this truth.

What we do know is that when we're having a bad day, we want to be excused by others. Isn't it a funny thing? We won't tolerate another's arrogance when they're having a bad day, but when we are, we act like we deserve all pardon.

It's comforting to know that the saints struggled with this too. St. Therese, known for her Little Way, recounts, "On another occasion when I was engaged in the laundry, the Sister opposite to me, who was washing handkerchiefs, kept splashing me continually with dirty water. My first impulse was to draw back and wipe my face in order to show her that I wanted her to be more careful. The next moment, however, I saw the folly of refusing treasures thus generously offered, and I carefully refrained from betraying any annoyance. On the contrary I made such efforts to welcome the shower of dirty water that at the end of half an hour I had taken quite a fancy to the novel kind of aspersion, and resolved to return as often as possible to the place where such precious treasures were freely bestowed."

Do we see how St. Therese turned this opportunity to be offended into an offering? What amazes me is that she made more efforts to go back. Imagine if we did that. Wouldn't our lives be more peaceful? Wouldn't we bring more peace to others?

Like St. Therese, we can grow in this grace and hopefully one day repeat what she said, "When things that are irritable or disagreeable befall me, instead of assuming an air of sadness, I respond by a smile. At first I was not always successful, but now it is a habit which I am very happy to have acquired."

It's important to make a note that mercy and forgiveness are aspects of love, and love always wants the ultimate good for another. Therefore, we must be careful that our mercy and forgiveness don't get twisted into something else and enable someone to continue destructive behavior. Today's culture has confused mercy with tolerance. We now tolerate behavior that is less than the dignity of the human person and call it mercy. On top of that, our culture doesn't want any pain or suffering. That makes it hard for mercy to be cultivated because sometimes mercy hurts. Mercy is again an aspect of love, which is always true. Truth and mercy go hand in hand. I think of my dad calling the cops on me. My teenage reaction said that wasn't merciful, but in truth, it was (regardless of what I thought!). My dad was showing me love and mercy by giving me boundaries and consequences to my bad and harmful behavior. My dad wanted what was good for me, the ultimate good. At the time I couldn't see it, but looking back, I recognize his love and how much it hurt him to do that act of mercy.

God our Father does the same. Giving his only son to die an excruciating death on the cross was the ultimate act of mercy because it saved us all. Jesus' death gives us eternal life. God willingly suffered so we could live.

We learn that we are to be stripped of ourselves so only Jesus remains, that we will fall and we must keep getting up, and most importantly, that we can give when we have nothing left. One way to meditate on the mercy given to us on the cross is to pray the Stations of the Cross. The more we grow in mercy, the more we grow in forgiveness. I encourage you to make the Stations of the Cross a regular part of your prayer schedule (weekly, bi-weekly or monthly). It will help us grow in mercy and forgiveness, which we need every day.

Lastly, we must forgive ourselves. Isn't it a paradox? When we want to be excused of wrongdoing, there are all the excuses in the world, but when we want to be forgiven of wrongdoing, we can't seem to find one excuse. Good thing there is one excuse and one remedy. It is Jesus. If you have been to confession, he has forgiven you. He took on our sin and paid the price for it on the cross, so that we would be free. You are no longer guilty. The devil will try to remind you of what you did. He will flash images of your former ways. If we didn't feel shame for them, our hearts would be hardened, so this is a healthy shame. But shame has its place to remind us of God's mercy, to praise him evermore and to live in the freedom Jesus won for us. Just as we are not to judge others, we are not to judge ourselves. All judging is up to God. God doesn't want us to be self-condemning. He wants us to live freely in his love. If you haven't done so already, give yourself to God to judge and say, "(**first, middle, last name**), I forgive you." Forgiving ourselves can seem harder than forgiving others, but when we do, we will experience a new peace and freedom. We will open a new channel of grace, and hang on, because God will overflow it. Our Lady also wants us to forgive ourselves. She said in part of one of her messages, "My children, I am here with you; I am next to you. I am showing you the way to forgive yourselves, to forgive others, and, with sincere repentance of heart, to kneel before the Father" (January 2, 2010).

"For as you judge, so will you be judged, and the measure with which you measure will be measured out to you" (Jesus - Matthew 7:2).

Questions for Your Personal Reflection

1. Have I truly forgiven my parents?
2. Whom am I holding grudges against? Who is someone I never want to see again?
3. Have I forgiven myself?

Questions for Small Group Discussion

1. How has having a forgiving heart changed my outlook?
2. What has surprised me about forgiveness?
3. When I sense myself becoming resentful, what are some strategies I have to transform that?

Action Item

Read "From Resentment to Forgiveness: A Gateway to Happiness" by Francisco Ugarte.

How much is too much?

Chapter 12

For many of us, tithing is a stumbling block. It's the part of our faith life that we still hold onto and want to control. We have surrendered to God our lives, our work, our families, our hearts, our everything, but not our bank accounts. For some reason it's easier to believe that we will have enough when it comes to the spiritual blessings, but when it comes to the material blessings, we don't think we will.

We know deep down we could be giving more. Deep down we want to give more, but we're afraid. We're afraid that we're going to give to God and he won't give back. We're afraid that what we give will be wasted. We're afraid we'll get the short end of the deal. We're afraid we won't have enough. That's what it all boils down to. Thank God, we have a Father who understands us — our frailty, our worries, and our lack of faith. Take a moment to call upon the Holy Spirit to open your heart and read the following passage slowly:

> Therefore I tell you, do not worry about your life, what you will eat [or drink], or about your body, what you will wear. Is not life more than food and the body more than clothing? Look at the birds in the sky; they do not sow or reap, they gather nothing into barns, yet your heavenly Father feeds them. Are not you more important than they? Can any of you by worrying add a single moment to your lifespan? Why are you anxious about clothes? Learn from the way the wildflowers grow. They do not

work or spin. But I tell you that not even Solomon in all his splendor was clothed like one of them. If God so clothes the grass of the field, which grows today and is thrown into the oven tomorrow, will he not much more provide for you, O you of little faith? So do not worry and say, 'What are we to eat?' or 'What are we to drink?' or 'What are we to wear?' All these things the pagans seek. Your Heavenly Father knows that you need them all. But seek first the kingdom [of God] and his righteousness, and all these things will be given you besides. Do not worry about tomorrow; tomorrow will take care of itself. Sufficient for a day is its own evil (Matthew 6:25-34).

Our Lady chose the passage above to be read and prayed with each week. She is helping us become less material and more spiritual.

While tithing appears to deal with the material, it is also very spiritual. As we grow in our spiritual life, we recognize ourselves decreasing and Jesus increasing. We recognize our nothingness in that we are nothing without him. Everything we have and are is from him. He is our everything. As these seeds take root, we see our former self-appointed role as "owner" of our material goods transformed into God's appointed role for us as "steward." The more God is everything, the more we want nothing. We begin to see that what God has blessed us with (even if very little) is meant to bless others. We see that God is asking us to trust him.

We are very private in the West when it comes to talking about money, especially personal finances. Our culture has been leading the world in consumerism and in the mentality that we should get what we want when we want it, even if we can't afford it. In essence, greed. This has stifled the spirit of tithing because we have grown accustomed to "getting our money's worth." We've come to scrutinize where our giving is going. What will it be used for? Who is in charge of it? Do I get a tax break? We don't trust that the beggar will buy food with it or the

Church will use it for evangelization. We think we're doing more for God by being "wise" with our money than giving it to those in need.

Tithing gives us those wings to trust God and to make an act of faith. We see a beautiful account of this in the Gospel of Mark, when Jesus observed how the crowd put money in the treasury. He saw many rich people put in large sums and then a poor widow who gave two small coins worth a few cents. "Calling his disciples to himself, he said to them, 'Amen, I say to you, this poor widow put in more than all the other contributors to the treasury. For they have all contributed from their surplus wealth, but she, from her poverty, has contributed all she had, her whole livelihood'" (Mark 12:42-44). Tithing, like our faith life, is a matter between God and ourselves. Just as Jesus knew the poor widow gave from her livelihood, he also knows today what we give from. We can ask ourselves, How often do we give from our surplus? How often do we give what we have "leftover," "worn-out," or "extra?" How often do we give from our livelihood? Do we give tithing a priority in our budget? We have to answer these questions for ourselves. And we shouldn't let the truth of our answers shame us, but rather shed light into a place we've kept God out of. We can acknowledge where we are and where we want to be.

So where do we want to be? We want God involved in our finances. We want to surrender control to him and let him be in charge. We want to be responsible stewards of the gifts he has given us. We want to give cheerfully and in secret. Like in all things, we want to glorify him.

It can simply begin by praying to invite God into your finances. To take inventory and talk to him about it as if he's sitting at the table with you (because he is) as you go through it. What is your yearly income, what is your debt, what is your budget (do you have a budget)? What is the whole picture of your personal financial state. A wonderful book to help you walk through this process is *The 21-Day Financial Fast*, by Michelle Singletary. My husband and I did the 21-day remedy she suggests, and it was transformative for our finances. Not only did we learn to aggressively pay down debt (within ten months, we owned both our cars), but we also learned to make tithing a priority budget item. You read a chapter a day and keep a short journal. Scripture is woven in, as well as personal testimonies. Throughout this process it became very clear that God wants us to be free, but many of us are still handcuffed because of debt, not properly managing our finances, and not being honest with ourselves about the reality of our financial state.

Growing in self-knowledge and truth are constant themes in the spiritual life, and that includes our personal finances. God cares about our finances. He wants to help us with them, but we can't let him if we don't know what specifically he's helping us with. How would we know that bonus we receive is to help pay off debt (not go on vacation) when we don't realize we have so much debt? How would we know that our beauty routines or supplies were taking up hundreds of dollars each month if we don't include them in the budget? We need the self-knowledge and truth of our finances. We need to start here so we can learn how to tithe.

Again, tithing is between God and ourselves. The origin of the word is "tenth," which goes back to the Old Testament when Abraham gave a tenth, hence tithe, of everything (Genesis 14:20). The Church teaches that we should tithe, and while 10% is mentioned in Scripture, the Church does not require a specific percentage or amount. We can learn from St. Paul who said, "So I thought it necessary to encourage the brothers to go on ahead to you and arrange in advance for your promised gift, so that in this way it might be ready as a bountiful gift and not as an exaction. Consider this: whoever sows sparingly will also reap sparingly, and whoever sows bountifully will also reap bountifully. Each must do as already determined, without sadness or compulsion, for God loves a cheerful giver. Moreover, God is able to make every grace abundant for you, so that in all things, always having all you need, you may have an abundance for every good work" (2 Corinthians 5-8). The Church also values our time and talent as contributions, not just our treasure.

Learning to tithe takes time. Identifying areas of spending for cut backs is a helpful part of the process. For example, when my husband and I saw how much we were paying for our cable and internet bill each month, we asked ourselves, Do we really need it? We prayed about it and decided to eliminate cable. We realized we could stream what we wanted on the Internet anyway. That decision alone saved us $130 a month. We then had the freedom to ask God what he wanted us to do with that savings.

One evening after dinner, Christian brought up tithing and said he had prayed, and knew what we were meant to do with that money. Meanwhile, I couldn't wait to tell Christian that I had also prayed and knew what we were meant to do with the money. It was beautiful because God spoke to us individually, but gave us the same message: we were to use that money to feed the poor. With that confirmation we set up a monthly donation to Mary's Meals, a wonderful non-profit that feeds more than one million children a day around the world in a place of education. Ninety-three percent of every dollar goes directly to feeding the children.

If you haven't been tithing, begin with the desire to tithe and take inventory of your personal finances. Look for areas to cut back. Pray and ask God what your tithe should be right now — not what it will be once such and such happens, but right now as it is.

If you have been tithing, I encourage you to take inventory of your personal finances again, with a prayerful heart look closely at the areas that could be cut back. Do you need the higher end model of the car? Is too much being spent on a hobby? You will know if something isn't settling right in your heart. Identify it and ask God what he wants you to do about it. Now this isn't saying that God doesn't want us to be blessed in this life. No, it's simply that he doesn't want us attached to this life. Jesus reminds us again and again, "No one can serve two masters. He will either hate one and love the other, or be devoted to one and despise the other. You cannot serve God and mammon" (Matthew

6:24). Also, "Jesus looked at him [now sad] and said, 'How hard it is for those who have wealth to enter the kingdom of God! For it is easier for a camel to pass through the eye of a needle than for a rich person to enter the kingdom of God'" (Luke 18:24-25). Let us pray that through our cutting back and tithing, we become poor in spirit.

I didn't expect this chapter to go into all of this. But the Holy Spirit is trying to wake us up. He's trying to get us out of debt, as Scripture tells us, "Owe nothing to anyone, except to love one another; for the one who loves another has fulfilled the law" (Romans 13:8). We cannot be free to love when we owe. The Holy Spirit is stirring us up to remind us that we can't take "things" to heaven. "Then he said to the crowd, 'Take care to guard against all greed, for though one may be rich, one's life does not consist of possessions'" (Jesus in Luke 12:15). He is showing us that he wants to be involved in our finances just as much as he wants to be involved in our family, our work, our leisure — our everything.

"Give and gifts will be given to you; a good measure, packed together, shaken down, and overflowing, will be poured into your lap. For the measure with which you measure will in return be measured out to you" (Luke 6:38).

Questions for Your Personal Reflection

1. Do I have a clear understanding of my personal finances? What can I do to start taking an inventory? Upon reflection, what does it say about where my heart is by where I spend my money?
2. How can I invite God into my finances? Do I feel God calling me about certain aspects of my time, talent, and treasure, or specific causes to support?

Question for Small Group Discussion

1. What has been particularly challenging for me in this topic?

Action Item
Try tithing 10% of your total income for just one month.

Mama!

Chapter 13

It seems a little odd to have a chapter on Our Lady considering her voice is throughout these pages and we already have a relationship with her. But it always pleases God when we praise him, especially for his most perfect creature, the Blessed Virgin Mary. So that's what we'll do in this chapter — Praise God by loving Mary.

"Dear children! I want you to understand that I am your Mother, that I want to help you and call you to prayer" (August 25, 1993). Our Lady couldn't say it more simply than that. In so many of her messages she reminds us that she's our mother, that she's helping us and she wants us to be holy for her son.

Our Lady is a creature, made by God, like all of us. She differs in being conceived without original sin, thus giving her the title Immaculate Mary. She always did and continues to do the will of God. She helps us to do the same. "Dear children! No, you don't know how to love, and you don't know how to listen with love to the words I am saying to you. Be conscious, my beloved, that I am your Mother, and I have come on earth to teach you to listen out of love, to pray out of love and not be compelled by the fact that you are carrying a cross. By means of the Cross God is glorified through every person. Thank you for having responded to my call" (November 29, 1984).

There is very little information about Our Lady in the Scriptures. Perhaps the most profound passage was when Jesus was dying on the cross: "When Jesus saw his mother and the disciple there whom he loved, he said to his mother, 'Woman, behold, your son.' Then he said to the disciple, 'Behold, your mother.' And from that hour the disciple took her into his home" (John 19:26-27). At that moment, Jesus gave every child of God his Mother as its own Mother. Mary is your Mother. She loves you, prays for you, intercedes for you, and she wants to draw you closer and closer to her son, Jesus. She is the most tender of all mothers and desires that all her children have eternal life.

In so many ways, it's difficult for me to find the words to describe my Heavenly Mother, as it is to describe my earthly mother. Sure, I could tell you of their traits, their tenderness and their love, but that doesn't capture them. It's because it's not just them I'm trying to describe; it's "us." It's the relationship I have with my earthly mother and my Heavenly Mother. In my earthly mother, I have learned so much about our Heavenly Mother. My earthly mother knows when something is wrong just by taking one look at me. She can tell when I'm starting to get sick (before I do in some cases). She sees my greatest strengths and understands my weaknesses. She knows my favorite things, and what gives me great joy and great sorrow. She always gives the best, most thoughtful gifts that leave me saying, "How did you know?" She knows how to comfort me, how to give pep talks and how to give me a nudge in the right direction. She knows how to call me out when I need a reality check. She understands things about me that I'm just discovering for myself. She would rather suffer herself than to see me suffer. She prays for me. She loves me. She will always love me. Our Heavenly Mother is like that and even more.

One way to grow in your relationship with Mary is through a consecration to her. This is a way of setting yourself apart for Our Lady, giving her everything you do and have (both spiritual and material) for her to use in the best possible way to glorify God. An authentic consecration to Our Lady always leads us to Jesus. In consecrating ourselves to Mary, we are giving everything to Jesus through her, just as God gave us Jesus through Mary. St. Louis de Montfort's consecration is absolutely beautiful and, though it is demanding because there are lengthy daily prayers for 33 days. If that seems too daunting, there is another in the book *33 Days to Morning Glory*, by Father Michael Gaitley. Begin here. In this way, you are inviting Our Lady to fully come into your life and take over. St. Louis de Montfort 's consecration talks of becoming slaves of Mary, and while that language may seem strong, it comes right from Scripture: "But now that you have been freed from sin and have become slaves of God, the benefit that you have leads to sanctification, and its end is eternal life" (Romans 6:22). This notion of slavery may be puzzling because we desire freedom, yet in our human nature, we end up being slaves to one thing or another. In being slaves to money, sex, alcohol, power, status, food and the like, we violate the First Commandment of "You shall not have other gods beside me" (Exodus 20:3). Jesus teaches us, "Amen, amen, I say to you, everyone who commits sin is a slave of sin" (Jesus, Matthew 8:34). When we sin we become a slave to sin, and when we're righteous we become a slave to holiness. Our actions decide which master we follow.

In lives of sinfulness and slavery to sin, the devil is at work and has more access to the person. There are varying degrees of the devil's influence in a person's life. Due to original sin, all of us experience oppression by the devil. Oppression includes daily temptations. Frequent reception of the sacraments, living in the grace of God, praying and not opening the door to the devil through the occult, are all ways to avoid sin. The next level of the devil's influence on a person is referred to as obsession. This is a choice. The person has to invite the devil in. It is most commonly experienced through the occult — especially magic, spiritism and satanism. Addiction and promiscuity are other footholds that the devil uses to enter more into a person. Lastly, there is possession. This is when a person has become possessed by the devil. They are no longer acting on their own, but rather as instruments of the devil.

So all this might be new to you or even a little frightening. Maybe you're afraid that you've invited the evil one into your life without realizing it. Do not fear. Mother Mary has been helping you. If you haven't confessed involvement with the occult, now is the time to do so. If you struggle with addiction or promiscuity or immodesty, bring it to confession again and again. By God's grace and mercy, and through the intercession of Our Lady, they will remove the devil's hold on your life. Msgr. Esseff said that a contrite confession is more powerful than an exorcism (because it is an act of the will, and confession is a sacrament given to us by Christ). Mother Mary goes into the depths of hell on earth and brings God's children to the light. You must remember that Mary is our Mother, but she is also extremely powerful. She crushes Satan's head with her heel. In an interview with the late Father Gabriel Amorth — who was the chief exorcist in Rome and who conducted more than 70,000 exorcisms during his priesthood — he was asked who was the most powerful intercessor of all. His response? "Of course, the Madonna is even more effective. Ah, when you invoke Mary!" Fr. Amorth goes on, "And, once I also asked Satan, 'but why are you more scared when I invoke Our Lady than when I invoke Jesus Christ?' He answered me, 'Because I am more humiliated to be defeated by a human creature than being defeated by him.'" [17]

It is Mary's humility that Satan's pride cannot stand.

In consecrating ourselves to Mother Mary, we are choosing and inviting her into our lives. We are asking her to take our actions and to make us instruments in her hands. When Mother Mary comes into our lives, she brings peace, joy, love, faith, and hope. She brings her son. When we enthrone Mary and Jesus in our hearts, we automatically dethrone the devil. Not only is a consecration to Mary a protection, but she also helps us become who God created us to be. On top of that, we get to help her in fulfilling God's plan. We ought to renew our consecration daily. As St. Louis de Monfort said, consecration to Mary is the "quickest, easiest, surest, and most perfect way" to sanctity.

It's hard to imagine, but even the best earthly mother doesn't compare

---

[17] David Kerr, "Rome's exorcist finding John Paul II effective against Satan," Catholic News Agency, last modified 17 May, 2011.
<http://www.catholicnewsagency.com/news/romes-exorcist-finding-bl.-john-paul-ii-effective-against-satan//>

to our Heavenly Mother. This is because we're talking about the Mother of our Savior Jesus Christ. God couldn't give his only son to any woman. In order to preserve Christ's holiness and sinlessness, he had to create a mother who was also sinless. Just as Mother Mary carried Christ in her womb for nine months and gave birth to him in the world, she now carries the Body of Christ (all of us) in her womb to be born into heaven. God chose Mary to be Jesus' vessel into and from this world. You might say, Wait. But didn't Jesus already ascend into heaven? And she wasn't his vessel then. How does this include us? The answer is in Scripture, which tells us that, "For as in one body we have many parts, and all the parts do not have the same function, so we, though many, are one body in Christ and individually parts of one another" (Romans 12:4-5).

> As a body is one though it has many parts, and all the parts of the body, though many, are one body, so also Christ . . . Now the body is not a single part, but many. If a foot should say, "Because I am not a hand I do not belong to the body," it does not for this reason belong any less to the body . . . If the whole body were an eye, where would the hearing be? If the whole body were hearing, where would the sense of smell be. But as it is, God placed the parts, each one of them, in the body as he intended . . . If [one] part suffers, all the parts suffer with it; if one part is honored, all the parts share its joy (1 Corinthians 12:12-26).

Mother Mary is most concerned with the eternal life of all God's children (just as Jesus is). Salvation comes to us through Jesus Christ, and that is why she is always drawing us closer to him.

One night in high school, I drank too much and was very sick. My parents unexpectedly picked me up and were in shock at the condition I was in. My mother slept next to me that night and while I don't remember much, I remember her telling me again and again, "I'm not giving up on you." I will never forget those words because I understand that both my mothers, earthly and heavenly, were telling me this, and it was the truth. Our Heavenly Mother says that to you too, no matter how far you've strayed, how much pain you're in or how shameful you are. Mother Mary remained at the foot of the cross of Jesus. Her heart is pierced. She understands suffering. Let her help you come back to Jesus.

Besides St. Louis de Montfort's consecration (renewed daily and the 33-days renewal annually), the other Marian devotion that's most powerful would have to be the rosary. I have also found the scriptural rosary helps me really enter into the mysteries and meditate on the life of Jesus. Again, through the rosary, Mary brings us closer to Jesus. Starting to pray the rosary takes patience and time. But don't let that stop you. Begin with one decade.

By beginning to pray to Mary, you will discover her role in your life. You've probably experienced her presence in a profound way in Medjugorje. Now that you're back, you will come across new devotions, books, and Marian retreats. All you have to do is say "Yes" to Mary. Your relationship with her will grow and develop, and it will be so personal. She invites us all to pray the rosary so that's why I've included it. But maybe some will make praying the Seven Sorrows of Mary a devotion, and others will live out the First Saturdays. Our Lady gave this devotion to Sister Lucia during the Fatima apparitions. Our Lady promised that she would, "assist at the hour of death with the graces necessary for salvation, all those who on the first Saturdays of five consecutive months confess, receive Holy Communion, pray a rosary, and keep me company for a quarter of an hour meditating on the 15 mysteries with the intention of offering reparation" for the sins committed against her Immaculate Heart and for peace.[18]

There is so much to choose from and you don't have to do it all. Find

---

[18] Michelle Laque Johnson, "Our Lady Requested First Saturday Devotions," EWTN, accessed 10 August, 2016. < http://www.ewtn.com/wings/2013/may2/wings0502Feature.htm>

something that speaks to you, and make it part of your prayer and life. It's just like children show their love for their mother in a variety of ways — hugs and kisses, flowers, phone calls, cards, and visits. Our Heavenly Mother loves being loved by each of us in our own way. Below I've included some Marian devotions given to us by the Church. There are some here that I am looking forward to learning more about too:

- Angelus (or replaced by the Regina Coeli during the Easter season)
- Brown Scapular
- Consecration to Mary
- Crowning of Mary
- Litany of Loretto
- Marian Apparitions (Medjugorje, Lourdes, Fatima, Guadalupe, Akita and more)
- Marian Processions
- Mary garden
- Miraculous Medal
- Month of May
- Novenas
- Reparation to the Immaculate Heart
- Rosary
- Seven Joys of Mary
- Seven Sorrows of Mary
- Saturdays (First Saturdays in a particular way)
- 3 Hail Marys at night before bed for the intention of purity

Our Lady will help us in our journey to continue following Jesus. She tells us, "Dear children! I am calling every one of you to start living in God's love. Dear children, you are ready to commit sin, and to put yourselves in the hand of Satan without reflecting. I call on each one of you to consciously decide for God and against Satan. I am your Mother and, therefore, I want to lead you all to perfect holiness. I want each one of you to be happy here on earth and to be with me in heaven. That is, dear children, the purpose of my coming here and it's my desire. Thank you for having responded to my call" (May 25, 1987). May you come to know the powerful intercession of Our Lady, her tender love for each of us, and the endless praise and thanksgiving we should give God for offering us his mother as our mother.

"And coming to her, he said, 'Hail, favored one! The Lord is with you.'" (Angel Gabriel to Mary in Luke 1:28).

Questions for Your Personal Reflection

1. How has Mother Mary been present in my life?
2. Am I aware of her loving me and helping me?
3. What is it that she's inviting me to? What can I do to help grow in my relationship with Mary?

Questions for Small Group Discussion

1. When did I first become aware of Mary's presence in my life?
2. It is said that every woman reveals a part of Mary. What Marian virtues or characteristics do you recognize in the women in your life? In yourself?
3. How do you envision growing in your relationship with Mary?

Action Item

Consecrate yourself to Mary using Fr. Michael Gaitley's "33 Days to Morning Glory" or St. Louis de Montfort's "Total Consecration to Jesus through Mary" (also 33 days).

For fun

Chapter 14

Now this is a fun chapter. These are some of the fruits I've experienced from living the five stones. When I started out, I didn't know what was ahead. The same is true for you. You've started this journey and you don't know what's ahead. Know though, that as you focus on living the five stones first, The Lord will show you the next step. He will lead you and He will make it clear. What comes after the five stones will be different for each one of us because it will be *your* individual path to holiness.

So do not be overwhelmed by this chapter in thinking you have to do it all, because you don't. I am simply sharing fruits with you so you can recognize the fruits in your life and see how God might be calling you. "The time each one of us has at his disposal is short, but long enough to tell God that we love Him and to accomplish the work He has given us" (*In Conversation with God* Volume 1-37.1).

We'll begin by acknowledging that it is a danger when we're satisfied with our faith life. It's a sign that we've stopped seeking more. And we know that we will not be complete until we see God face to face. When we're at a standstill, it's usually because we've fallen a little out of love with our Creator. Love always brings newness to relationships, including our relationship with God. The words of Father Pedro Arrupe, SJ can help us out:

Nothing is more practical than
finding God, than
falling in Love

in a quite absolute, final way.
What you are in love with,
what seizes your imagination, will affect everything.
It will decide
what will get you out of bed in the morning,
what you do with your evenings,
how you spend your weekends,
what you read, whom you know,
what breaks your heart,
and what amazes you with joy and gratitude.
Fall in Love, stay in love,
and it will decide everything.

The following topics are some reminders that can reignite the fire — the burning desire to love and serve God. We all need this at some point. They are:

- Spiritual direction
- Devotion to the Holy Souls in Purgatory
- Spiritual reading and listening
- Attending a "Life in the Spirit" seminar
- Going on a retreat or to a conference
- Completing Works of Mercy
- Praying for priests

Spiritual Direction

At some point in our lives, we have been coached, tutored, taught or mentored — whether for school, sports or hobbies. So it is only natural that we receive direction in our faith journey as well. The reason is that it's easy to deceive ourselves. It's easy for us to think we're one way, but in reality act another. It's easy to get caught up in our thoughts and to think at one level. St. John of the Cross said, "The virtuous soul that is alone and without a master [a spiritual director] is like a burning coal; it will grow colder rather than hotter."

The overall role of the spiritual director is to help us grow in our relationship with God. It can be manifested in many ways, and each director/directee relationship is unique to that directee's soul. In my experience, a spiritual director helps us see ourselves in a new perspective (and hopefully more like how God sees us). They are able to recognize themes in our spiritual life and help us link them together so we can better understand what God is speaking to us. They are able to make recommendations that we can apply in a practical way to our spiritual life. They can answer questions, or direct us to people or places for the answers. They can teach us how to have a richer and deeper faith life.

I think one of the greatest examples of a spiritual director comes right out of Scripture. It is the Ethiopian eunuch's story in the Acts of the Apostles. The passage says,

"So he got up and set out. Now there was an Ethiopian eunuch, a court official of the Candace, that is, the queen of the Ethiopians, in charge of her entire treasury, who had come to Jerusalem to worship, and was returning home. Seated in his chariot, he was reading the prophet Isaiah. The Spirit said to Philip, 'Go and join up with that chariot.' Philip ran up and heard him reading Isaiah the prophet and said, 'Do you understand what you are reading?' He replied, 'How can I, unless someone instructs me?' So he invited Philip to get in and sit with him" (Acts 8:27-31).

Philip instructs the eunuch about the Scriptures, which then leads the eunuch to ask, "Look, there is water. What is to prevent my being baptized?" (Acts 8:36). This encounter leaves the eunuch rejoicing because he has been baptized in Christ. Spiritual directors, like Philip, are simply instruments in God's hands. They lead their directees, like the eunuch, to Christ.

A spiritual director can be a priest, religious brother or sister, deacon, consecrated virgin or even a layperson. Finding one can take time and patience. Pray. Pray. Pray. Don't be surprised if it's someone you wouldn't expect, but also make sure they've had training as a spiritual director. Getting into a regular meeting schedule with a spiritual director is also very helpful. Sometimes we go to them for a period of time and then we go without for awhile. There is no right or wrong way. It is what you and your spiritual director decide. Another note, if you find that don't you "click" with your spiritual director, it's okay to find a different one.

Start praying for your spiritual director now, and if you have one that you haven't seen in awhile, set up another meeting.

Devotion to the Holy Souls in Purgatory

We'll start by traveling with St. Faustina to purgatory:

> " . . . [The next night] I saw my Guardian Angel, who ordered me to follow him. In a moment I was in a misty place full of fire in which there was a great crowd of suffering souls. They were praying fervently, but to no avail, for themselves; only we can come to their aid. The flames which were burning them did not touch me at all. My Guardian Angel did not leave me for an instant. I asked these souls what their greatest torment was. They answered me in one voice that their greatest torment was longing for God. I saw Our Lady visiting the souls in purgatory. The souls call her 'The Star of the Sea.' She brings them refreshment. I wanted to talk with them some more, but my Guardian Angel beckoned me to leave. We went out of that prison of suffering. [I heard an interior voice] which said, 'My mercy does not want this, but justice demands it.' Since that time, I am in closer communion with the suffering souls." [19]

While this is a short selection, it is packed with the necessary details of why the souls in Purgatory need our prayers. We learn that these souls

---

[19] Saint Faustina, Diary of Saint Maria Faustina Kowalska: Divine Mercy in My Soul (Stockbridge, MA: Marian Press, 2005), 11.

pray fervently, but to no avail for themselves. It is our prayers that help them. St. Alphonsus Ligouri beautifully reiterated this point when he said, "Though the Holy Souls cannot merit for themselves, they can obtain for us great graces. They are not, formally speaking, intercessors as the saints are but, through the sweet providence of God, they can obtain for us outstanding favors and deliver us from evils, sickness and dangers of every kind."

These Holy Souls are part of the Body Christ. They are part of the Church. They are part of our faith journey because we are part of the Body of Christ. We are part of the Church. The more we travel along our faith journey, the more we realize the unity of the Body of Christ; the more charity grows in our hearts for our neighbors; and the more compassion grows in our souls for the suffering of others.

One time in 1983, the children asked Our Lady about Purgatory and this is what she said,

> There are different levels of which the lowest are close to Hell and the highest gradually draw near to Heaven. It is not on All Souls day, but at Christmas, that the greatest numbers of souls leave Purgatory. Those in Purgatory are the souls who pray ardently to God, but for whom no relative or friend prays for them on earth. God makes them benefit from the prayers of other people. It happens that God permits them to manifest themselves in different ways, close to their relatives on earth, in order to remind men of the existence of Purgatory, and to solicit their prayers close to God who is just, but good. The majority go to Purgatory. Many go to Hell. A small number go directly to Heaven.[20]

Our Lady of Medjugorje also said in one of her messages on November

---

[20] "Concordance of Our Lady's Messages 1981-2014," Medjugorje Web, accessed 5 June, 2016. <https://www.medjugorje.org/concordance/framconc.htm>

6, 1986:

> Dear children! Today I wish to call you to pray daily for souls in purgatory. For every soul, prayer and grace are necessary to reach God and the love of God. By doing this, dear children, you obtain new intercessors who will help you in life to realize that all the earthly things are not important for you, that only heaven is that for which it is necessary to strive. Therefore, dear children, pray without ceasing that you may be able to help yourselves and the others to whom your prayers will bring joy. Thank you for having responded to my call.

We can begin by praying the St. Gertrude prayer for the Holy Souls. Our Lord told her that it would release 1,000 souls from purgatory each time it is prayed. It also includes prayers for sinners among the living. The prayer is:

Eternal Father, I offer thee the Most Precious Blood of thy Divine Son, Jesus, in union with the Masses said throughout the world today, for all the Holy Souls in Purgatory, for sinners everywhere, for sinners in the universal church, those in my own home and within my family. Amen.

Sometimes you'll find yourself thinking of someone who passed away years ago. Use this opportunity to pray for them. Bring your intention for the Holy Souls to Mass. You can even offer Masses for them. According to many saints, offering mass for the Holy Souls is the most effective means for their release.

I'd like to end with another quote from Our Lady of Medjugorje when the visionaries asked her about purgatory:

"There are different levels of which the lowest are close to hell and the highest gradually draw near to heaven. It is not on All Souls Day, but at Christmas, that the greatest numbers of souls leave purgatory. Those in purgatory are the souls who pray ardently to God, but for whom no relative or friend prays for them on earth. God makes them benefit from the prayers of other people. It happens that God permits them to manifest themselves in different ways, close to their relatives on earth, in order to remind men of the existence of purgatory, and to solicit their prayers close to God who is just, but good. The majority go to purgatory. Many go to hell. A small number go directly to heaven."

These holy souls in purgatory need our prayers. Let us begin today.

Spiritual Reading and Listening

When I was speaking with a confessor about writing this book, his first question was, "Do you read a lot?" He went on to say that one cannot write if one isn't reading. This really stuck with me because I realized I could be reading more. I think most of us want to be reading more, even if we're not writing. Reading opens up our minds and, before long, we start to see connections between what we're reading in one place and in another, although they may be completely unrelated.

Spiritual reading is another touch point we give God to speak to us. Finding a regular time to read each day can be helpful. Father Larry Richards has a motto, "Bible before breakfast." Reading Scripture each day is a good place to start, as Jesus also tells us that man cannot live on bread alone but every word that comes from the mouth of God.

By having an open ear to what he's inviting us to read can be transformative. It could be as simple as you overhearing two people talk about St. Gerard Majella while leaving Mass, and a little light goes off to look up whom that saint is. Turns out he's the patron of expectant mothers (and you're expecting). Or maybe a friend says you'd really enjoy *The Lamb's Supper* by Scott Hahn. Or you see a link in an article for *Imitation of Christ*, by Thomas à Kempis, online for free. Sometimes there won't be external promptings, but they'll come from inside, from the Holy Spirit. Perhaps you'll notice a new desire to know the *Catechism of the Catholic Church* better. Read a couple pages each day. Another wonderful resource is *In Conversation with God*, by

Francis Fernandez, which is a series of books of beautiful reflections based on the daily Mass readings.

The breadth and depth of spiritual reading and listening available to us is unfathomable. So boredom can't be an excuse to stop reading. Some days *The Dialogues* by St. Catherine of Siena speak directly to me, while other days I have no idea what it means. One topic I've found that never gets dull is reading about people's conversion and reconversion stories to Catholicism. There is always something profound about how an encounter with Christ transforms a person, and that always beautifully reminds me of when he called me.

Spiritual listening includes music. Exploring traditional Catholic liturgical music and chants is a wonderful practice. Podcasts can also be spiritual listening. On www.discerninghearts.com there are a variety of meditations, book reviews and interviews that are all geared toward those on the "discerning journey."

We are still on our faith journey, which means we are still students. By reading and listening to spiritual works, we are in the classroom.

Attending a "Life in the Spirit" Seminar

Something that continues to come up in my faith journey is how little I know about the Holy Spirit. Just when I think I have an understanding of his working or power, he surprises me and I realize I have just scratched the surface. He, being God, is a mystery, ever ancient and ever new. Being so humble, the Holy Spirit often remains hidden as he works in our lives. As a priest once said, "If you want to get wet, then you have to go where it's raining." The Holy Spirit is also raining in the Charismatic Renewal in the Catholic Church. The Holy Spirit is working wonders because he is called upon.

I didn't know what to think of the Charismatic Renewal when I first heard about it just a few years ago. It surprised me to know that people still prayed in tongues, and that they were prayed over and prophesizing.

I guess I had never really taken St. Paul's words seriously when he said, "Pursue love, but strive eagerly for the spiritual gifts, above all that you may prophesy. For one who speaks in a tongue does not speak to human beings but to God, for no one listens; he utters mysteries in spirit" (1 Corinthians 14:1-2). I get it that the Charismatic Renewal seems to be in left field from the traditional conservative Catholic Church we've grown accustomed to, but it's nonetheless part of our Church and faith. Pope Saint John Paul II said on December 11, 1979 to the international leaders of the Renewal, "I am convinced that this movement is a very important component of the entire renewal of the Church."

A "Life in the Spirit" seminar is a blessed reintroduction to the Holy Spirit, as well as a renewal of baptismal promises. It consists of six gatherings, usually in the evenings, that include Scripture, prayer, inspiring talks, and small groups. While that's the more practical side, a "Life in the Spirit" seminar helps us discover and develop our personal gifts of the Holy Spirit. We grow in a deeper relationship with the Holy Spirit and learn what God is calling us to do with our gifts and talents. We grew up knowing the Holy Spirit, but after this seminar, we *know* the Holy Spirit. It will probably move you out of your comfort zone. Not probably, it will. This can be so important to our faith journey because we need to be stirred up and we need to be reminded that we don't have it all figured out. God's ways must above all be our ways. We need to learn how to live in the Spirit. A "Life in the Spirit" seminar teaches us how to do that. Our Lady also reminds us to pray to the Holy Spirit in her messages. She says to pray to him every day to descend upon us. She tells us, "When one has him [the Holy Spirit], one has everything. People make a mistake when they turn only to the saints to request something" (October 21, 1983).

Who wouldn't want the fruits of the Holy Spirit? Love, joy, peace, patience, kindness, generosity, faithfulness, gentleness, and self-control (Galatians 5:22-23) — these are all infused graces that help us become saints. We need them, but more importantly, we need the source of them; we need the Holy Spirit.

Before discounting this idea, give it a try.

Going on a Retreat or to a Conference

Sometimes we need to get away. We need a change of scenery. We need to seek God in a new place and in a new way. Most times, we just need some peace and quiet to be with him and listen. Retreats and conferences provide this opportunity. While there are many Christian retreats offered, it is important to attend Catholic retreats and conferences so we can be with Jesus in the sacraments.

Retreats are designed for a more personal encounter with the Lord. While retreats can be either silent or not, they offer lots of time for prayer and reflection and, of course, Holy Mass and confession. Conferences, on the other hand, are usually not silent. Many of them offer opportunities for the sacraments, but the schedule is pretty full with speakers, so there isn't much time for personal prayer and reflection.

Retreats can be anywhere from one day to overnight for three, ten, or even more days. Conferences tend to be three days maximum. Both give us the opportunity to seek God more earnestly and receive graces. Setting aside the time for them isn't easy, especially with work and family schedules (yet it's easy for us to book a golf or spa weekend with friends). Choosing to give a weekend fully to God is a prayer in itself, and it is pleasing to him. Know that even when you book a retreat or a conference, something will come up to try to force you to cancel. Remember that the evil one doesn't want you to go deeper into your relationship with God.

Having been on a number of retreats and conferences, I would like to share five tips that have helped make them more fruitful for me. First, bring your Bible and journal. Second, take the necessary time and prayer to prepare for confession. Third, do not hold anything back, especially if you get to meet with a spiritual director. If you're going on retreat with something heavy on your heart, know that God wants to work it out with you. He probably called you on this retreat for this very reason. Fourth, sacrifice a little sleep. I'm not talking hours, but stay up later, get up earlier or get up in the night to be with our Lord in front of the tabernacle or Monstrance if they have perpetual Adoration. Fifth, make resolutions, but only a maximum of three. For each resolution, be sure not only to determine what it is, but how you'll implement it as well. For example, it's not enough to write, "Be more patient." You need to specify ways you'll practice more patience.

Sometimes the fruits of the retreats aren't apparent until much later, but don't let that discourage you. God is always at work in our favor. Adding a yearly retreat to our calendar opens up many graces in our life. Start now, and get one on the calendar.

Completing Works of Mercy

This section should be a given, considering it's living the Gospel, but it's worth the reminder nonetheless.

What's beautiful about the Spiritual and Corporal Works of Mercy is that they are specific. They're not "be good," "be nice," "be kind." God knows us. He knows that we'd be patting ourselves on the back satisfied we're all those things. The Works of Mercy give us specific deeds.

We can and should be asking ourselves:

Are we feeding the hungry?
Giving drink to the thirsty?
Clothing the naked?
Visiting the sick?
Visiting the imprisoned?
Burying the dead?
Giving alms to the poor?
Counseling the doubtful?

Instructing the ignorant?
Admonishing the sinner?
Comforting the sorrowful?
Forgiving injuries?
Bearing wrongs patiently?
Praying for the living and the dead?

The Lord uses a parable to tell us, "Amen, I say to you, whatever you did for one of these least brothers of mine, you did for me" (Matthew 25:40). This should be enough to get us on our feet and into action. In an interview, St. Mother Teresa said that all the people she cares for are Jesus in disguise. Imagine if we lived with that same mentality? Would we not automatically respond with Works of Mercy to all those in need?

This concept helps us realize that we often think the Works of Mercy come first, and that compassion and love will follow. No, it's the opposite. When we have compassion and love, then the Works of Mercy follow. We need more love, and that's what our faith journey is all about. Let us ask Jesus to give us his heart and his eyes to see the needs of our brothers and sisters, and respond with works. "See how a person is justified by works and not by faith alone" (James 2:24). May we see Jesus in disguise in all those we encounter. Our Lady also encourages us to do the Works of Mercy: "Dear children! Today I invite you to do works of mercy with love and out of love for me and for your and my brothers and sisters. Dear children, all that you do for others, do it with great joy and humility for God. I am with you, and day after day I offer your sacrifices and prayers to God for the salvation of the world. Thank you for having responded to my call" (November 25, 1990).

Praying for Priests

A priest once said in his homily that he'd like to make a bumper sticker that says, "No priests, no Eucharist." This is the truth. Without priests we do not have the Eucharist or the other sacraments. Priests have been chosen by Jesus Christ, ordained and entrusted with this great responsibility, yet they are still men, still human and still sinners. If we think we are fighting an intense spiritual battle, imagine what it's like for them. Our priests need our prayers. Much has been given to them and much will be required of them.

I grew in my devotion of praying for priests after reading how many times Our Lady reminds us to pray for them. "Pray for priests. My Son gave them to you as a gift" (May 2, 2008). She tells us that they hold a special place in her heart. She also tells us that we cannot do it without them, and she even cautions us not to judge them because her Son chose them (July 02, 2012). These are essential reminders. Our priests need our prayers — not our feedback on the homily, nor our complaints about the music, nor our judgment about their reverence. They need only our prayers.

Our Lady also reminds us about the power of a priest's blessing. Our Lady was described by one of the visionaries once as, "With a serious expression on her face, she [Our Lady of Medjugorje] emphasized once again the priestly blessing. With pain and love she said: 'Remember my children; that is my son blessing you. Do not accept this so lightly'" (June 2, 2006). It makes me think, how many times are our minds wandering during that final blessing at Mass? Let us take to heart Our Lady's words, and be attentive and accepting of priestly blessings.

We could also pray St. Therese of Lisieux's prayer for priests every day:

O Jesus, eternal Priest, keep your priests within the shelter of your Sacred Heart, where none may touch them. Keep unstained their anointed hands, which daily touch your Sacred Body. Keep unsullied their lips, daily purpled with your Precious Blood. Keep pure and unearthly their hearts, sealed with the sublime mark of the priesthood. Let your holy love surround them and shield them from the world's contagion. Bless their labors with abundant fruit and may the souls to whom they minister be their joy and consolation here and in heaven their beautiful and everlasting crown. Amen.

Questions for Your Personal Reflection

1. What have I been invited to or heard recently that caught my attention at first regarding my spiritual life, but then I ignored it?
2. Who would also enjoy a retreat or conference? (Invite them!)
3. What are two specific resolutions I want to make after reading this chapter?
4. When will I pray for my parish priest(s) each day?

Questions for Small Group Discussion

1. Which subsection of this chapter really stood out to you and why?
2. Can you give a personal experience to any of the subsections?
3. Is there something not listed here that you've been praying or thinking about?

Action Item

Complete a work of mercy as a group.

Conclusion

Here we are at the conclusion of the book. While it may seem like the end, we are actually at the beginning. This is the commissioning. Now is the time to put into practice what you read. Now is the time to stop worrying. Now is the time to really accept Our Lady's messages and live them. You are not alone in doing so. Millions of pilgrims have traveled to Medjugorje, whether physically or spiritually. You are home now, and the seed must grow where it is planted.

I'd like to share one final story.

One Monday evening a couple years ago, my husband and I were leaving a Bible study group from our parish. My husband likes to note that it was because he rambled towards the end that we left a little later than normal. I gave him a little trouble about it. As we were driving out of the parking lot, we passed the school behind the church. At that moment, a young man came out, sat down on the steps and buried his head in his hands.

I said to my husband, "We should ask him if he's ok." My husband was driving and kept going, saying, "He's probably fine. There are lights on at the school and there are probably lots of people in there. Maybe he just needed fresh air."

But the Holy Spirit wouldn't let me drop it. "We need to go back and ask him. It's just one question!" My husband kept driving. "Come on Darc. I'm sure he's fine." We had been driving a few minutes at this point. I continued, "We just came from Bible study! Are we going to live what we've learned or what?! We are disciples of Christ!"

My husband turned around. "Ok, but I'm going to pull up so he's on YOUR side, so you can talk to him." In those few minutes driving back, I prayed to the Holy Spirit for his words. As we pulled up, the young man was in the same position as when we left.

I rolled down my window, "Excuse me, are you ok?" He responded, "Oh yeah, I'm fine." I continued, "No really. I just had my husband turn around so we could come back to ask you if you're ok. Are you ok?" He cracked a smile and shook his head, "It's an AA meeting in the school and I had to take a break because so much was coming up."

At that moment, I knew exactly why God sent us to him. Only God would know to send a former alcohol abuser to this young man. I said, "I know how hard that is for you. I struggled with alcohol in high school and college. I know the pain, suffering, fear and desperation. You know what really helped me? Confession. Being able to bring all the shame, guilt, and regret to God for forgiveness and healing made such a difference. It changed my life. Are you Catholic?"

He answered, "Well yes, but kinda practicing." I couldn't believe I was being so bold — this was all the Holy Spirit! I asked, "Have you been to confession?"

He looked down, "No" and after a deep breath looked up and said, "You don't understand, I was just sitting here contemplating whether I should go to confession. I was looking up at the cross on top of the church and asking God. And then you guys come out of nowhere and you're telling me about confession. I can't believe this. Who are you?"

"I'm Darcie and this is Christian." At this point were both out of the car and shaking our new friend Gino's hand. We exchanged a few more words, gave him a hug and assured him of our prayers for him. He was in shock and all he could say was thank you. As we got back in the car, we could see him tearing up ... but he was smiling. He just had a God moment!

Driving home, Christian said, "I will never doubt you again" — but it's the Holy Spirit we'll never doubt again. I had never felt like such an instrument in God's hands as I did that night. It was beautiful!

There is nothing more beautiful than being an instrument in God's hand and that is my prayer for you. Being on the narrow path is difficult, but we have all the help of heaven.

When I was praying and entrusting this book to Our Lady, she told me that *she knew exactly whose lives this book would touch.* If you are reading this, you are one of them. Sometimes the greatest blessings are at the very end, hidden and discreet. Consider this a gift from your Heavenly Mother. Ask her what she wants you to do with it.

"Rejoice in the Lord always. I shall say it again: rejoice! Your kindness should be known to all. The Lord is near. Have no anxiety at all, but in everything, by prayer and petition, with thanksgiving, make your requests known to God. Then the peace of God that surpasses all understanding will guard your hearts and minds in Christ Jesus. Finally, brothers, whatever is true, whatever is honorable, whatever is just, whatever is pure, whatever is lovely, whatever is gracious, if there is any excellence and if there is anything worthy of praise, think about these things" (Philippians 4:4-8).

Epilogue

In the Scripture passage "On the Road to Emmaus," there are two men walking, one named Cleopas and other unnamed. I was the unnamed disciple. I was walking on the Road to Emmaus, away from Jerusalem — from faith, from God, from church. Then "Jesus himself drew near and walked with them" (Luke 24:15). My eyes were prevented from seeing him, but he taught me about the Scriptures. I asked him to stay with me. He broke bread for me. At that, my eyes were opened and I recognized him. I said, "Were not our hearts burning [within us] while he spoke to us on the way and opened the scriptures to us?" (Luke 24:32). I set out at once to return to Jerusalem. This book is my sharing of my encounter with Jesus, the Risen Lord.

Each of us is the unnamed disciple on the Road to Emmaus. Jesus draws near to each of us. He interprets the Scriptures for us. He breaks bread for us. We recognize him. We are forever changed. Our hearts burn within us. We return to Jerusalem and we share our encounter with him to all. We each have a call from him.

Acknowledgments

This book would not have been possible without the grace of God, the power of the Holy Spirit and the intercession of Our Lady. So to them, I offer my utmost thanksgiving and praise. To my husband, Christian, who believed I had something to share and kept encouraging me to write. Please thank him if you see him because he made this book possible, along with the sacrifices to write it. Thank you, my love. To my daughter, Mariella, who constantly reminds me to live in the present, to love and to enjoy God's love for us. To Zelie, who was in the womb when I wrote this, and how much I felt we were working on this book together. I love you both! With great affection, a sincere thank you to my parents. We have been through a lot! You are so dear to me and words can never express how much I love you and how grateful I am for you. To my brother, Maximilian, there are no words, I know you know. I have only one thing to tell you: your turn. To my extended family (grandparents, godparents, aunts, uncles, cousins, second cousins), thank you for teaching me what family is about. Thank you for your support, prayers, and love. To Mother Olga Yaqob and the Daughters of Mary of Nazareth, thank you for welcoming me into the community, for your prayers, and your commitment to religious life. Monsignor Esseff, I will forever thank God for you and your vocation. Thank you to all the priests who have administered the sacraments to me. Thank you for shepherding souls to Christ. To the St. Mary's community, especially my lovely friends at daily Mass, thank you for your prayers and friendship. To my dear friends, you know who you are, thank you for your love and support. To my phenomenal editors: Mary, Karen, Victoria, Laura and Ellen, thank you with all my heart. I also thank my many brothers and sisters in Christ who have journeyed with me, either since the beginning or for a period of time, or who are now or will be with me in the future. And for you, dear reader, thank you for taking the time to read this book. Praise be Jesus and Mary now and forever.

To get in touch or read more of my writing please visit: mysoulproclaims.org

Coming Home is available on Amazon.